a 30-day guide to

1 be-ing

a living thing: PERSON

conscious existence: LIFE

who God created you to be

by corey tabor
foreword by Pastor Gaylon Clark

This is what we speak, not in words taught us by human wisdom but in words taught by the Spirit, expressing spiritual truths in spiritual words.
1 Corinthians 2:13

Be Chosen

We want to hear from you. Please send your comments about this book to us at contact@iiicoaching.com. Thank you.

COACHING ™

[1]Be-ing
A 30-Day Guide to Being Who God Created You to Be.

Copyright © 2008 by Corey Tabor

This title is also available as an III Coaching audio book and e-book. Visit www.iiicoaching.com for more information.

Requests for books and additional information should be addressed to:
III Coaching, LLC
P.O. Box 972
Cedar Park, Texas 78630

All scripture quotations, unless otherwise indicated, are taken from the *Holy Bible: New International Version*®. NIV®. Copyright © 1973, 1978, 1984 International Bible Society. Used by permission of Zondervan Publishing House. All rights reserved.

All entries, pronunciations, functions and definitions, are taken from Merriam-Webster Online Dictionary copyright © 2005 by Merriam-Webster, Incorporated

Cover and Inside Design: Corey Tabor
Photography: Nycole Robertson – www.imagesbynycole.com
Editorial Assistance by Vanessa Paige Kirk
Website by Masudi Stolard – www.whogavetheorder.com

ISBN – 13: 978-0-9819377-0-0

Printed in the United States by Morris Publishing
3212 East Highway 30
Kearney, NE 68847
1-800-650-7888

Dedication

To April, my wife, my partner, my friend:
Thank you for creating an environment where I can fully
be who God created me to be. I look forward to
continuing our journey together.

Contents

Acknowledgments

I would like to greatly appreciate and honor . . .

My wife – April who inspires me to be a better man each day. I am so glad that God brought us together and I am so excited about His plan for our lives.

My parents – Pastor Samuel and Carrie Tabor for raising me to be a godly man. Thank you for modeling faithfulness to Christ and leading me to trust Him as my Savior.

My brother – Samuel Tabor for always believing in me.

My Pastor – Gaylon Clark for being a great example. Thank you for being a wonderful model, mentor and friend. I am forever indebted to you for your investment in me.

My Church Family – Greater Mt. Zion for giving me a safe place to grow as a pastor, teacher and leader.

My Mentors – Brian Wallace & David Hanke for giving me my first official ministry role with InterVarsity Christian Fellowship. Thanks for trusting and training me to lead.

My Mentor – Rodney Walker for believing in me and reminding me that God would always be with me.

My Mentor – Herman Hicks for modeling manhood for a young teenager who needed to see multiple examples.

InterVarsity Staff Team – For teaching me the value of discipleship and reconciliation.

Texas Gospel Fellowship – For teaching me to trust God beyond what I could see.

Foreword

PICTURE THIS! YOU OWN A FOOTBALL TEAM. YOU DRAFT players for your team who can't run fast enough, who are not very strong, and who have a history of underachieving. Yet in spite of their bio, you sign them to your team, give them a huge signing bonus, and put them in uniform. Why would you do this? You value who they are more than what they do!

There is absolutely nothing we have done to deserve being drafted by God. *But God demonstrates his own love for us in this: While we were still sinners, Christ died for us* (Romans 5:8).

Too often we base our identity on what we do on the field – how many touchdowns we run or tackles we make. The tension to perform is high with this approach to live! Our worth is measured more accurately by the sacrifices God made to include us on the team. Who we are is far more important to Him than what we do!

In this devotional guide, Corey Tabor, reminds us that "being" is a higher value than "doing." He explores our signing bonus as Christians and urges us to enjoy it. In fact, it's only when we enjoy who we are that we accomplish more for God. Remember God changed our identity before He addressed our behavior.

Pastoring a growing church has allowed me an audience with many gifted men and women of God. There is no one whose walk with God I respect more than Corey Tabor. I have learned from his journey with Christ. I know you will too!

Gaylon Clark
Lead Pastor
Greater Mount Zion Baptist Church
Austin, Texas

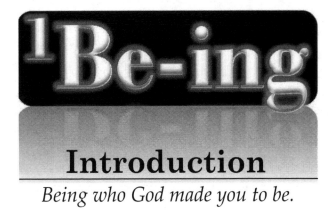

Introduction

Being who God made you to be.

DO YOU REMEMBER LEARNING AS A CHILD THE VALUE of self-actualization? I am sure you did not know how to say, or pronounce the word, but you were consistently asked the fundamental question of self-actualization, "What do you want to be when you grow up?" The question was a trick question. Because while being asked what you wanted to be, you were really being asked, "What do you want to do that will earn you a living so you can get off your parent's tab?"

We spend our entire lives meeting people and asking the question, "What do you do for a living?" So many people are productive, driven, seemingly successful, and yet unhappy because they have been answering the wrong question all along. The best question to ask is not, "What do you do for a living?" but rather, *"What are you being as you live?"* You can have a job that pays well, but does not allow you to fulfill your purpose.

Once you learn how to be who God created you to be, you can learn how to do what God created you to do out of your being.

11

Read Luke 10:38-41

38 As Jesus and his disciples were on their way, he came to a village where a woman named Martha opened her home to him. 39 She had a sister called Mary, who sat at the Lord's feet listening to what he said. 40 But Martha was distracted by all the preparations that had to be made. She came to him and asked, "Lord, don't you care that my sister has left me to do the work by myself? Tell her to help me!"

41 "Martha, Martha," the Lord answered, "you are worried and upset about many things, 42 but few things are needed—or indeed only one. Mary has chosen what is better, and it will not be taken away from her."

In this passage, we read about Mary and Martha, who are two sisters who sincerely love Jesus. Martha chose to do something for Jesus by making preparations for Him to be in her home, while Mary chose to be with Jesus to make preparations for what she would eventually *do*. Later in Scripture, we read of Mary giving one of the greatest sacrificial gifts described in the Bible. She poured a jar of perfume on Jesus that was equal to the value of a year's wages, because she had *been* with Jesus instead of just *doing* for Jesus. Mary gave a gift that was a reflection of her generosity, a gift birthed in a personal relationship defined by being *with* Christ. Similarly, what we do will flow out of who we are.

Earlier this year, I was leaving to go to work one day when a woman I had never met before asked me, "Do you ever slow down?" I was shocked at her candor and boldness. I was embarrassed of my lifestyle because though she had never met me, she knew me through observation from afar. I immediately began to defend myself listing all the reasons I needed to live at the pace I was living. She answered, "I used to run the rat race too. About two years ago, I just had to make a decision to slow down." With that, she left me to my own thoughts and drove away.

Driving down the freeway I could not seem to get her question out of my mind. I knew that God was trying to tell me something, but I was not ready to listen. So, when I arrived at work, one of my co-workers asked me, "Why are you here? You are not going to get anything done. Go home!" So after 30-minutes of driving to work thinking about the first conversation and 30-minutes of driving home thinking about the second conversation, I knew God was trying to tell me something and I started to listen.

That infamous day began a season of involuntary rest through the vehicle of burnout and fatigue. I could not think, I could not produce, and I could not function. My mind, body and spirit were burned out from living a Martha lifestyle. I was waking up at 6:00am and working until 12:00am trying to balance marriage, ministry and school. This Martha lifestyle kept me from sitting at the feet of Jesus. After six weeks of lying on my back, living from the bed to the couch, I finally learned that God is more concerned about who I am than what I can do for Him. I learned that being God's son is more important to my identity than being God's servant. This book is a response to my new life in Christ – being instead of doing.

In this book, you will learn to embrace life-changing character qualities that will help you *be* who God created you to be, so that you can *do* what God created you to do. Our character is defined by who we are, and who we are enables us to do what we do. For example, *being accepted* by God allows me to take the risk of sharing my faith. No matter how any individual responds, I am already accepted as God's child. *Being different* allows me to celebrate the uniqueness of others. When I know God has created me uniquely, I can embrace His unique creation in others. This is just the tip of the iceberg.

Each day you will focus an attribute that God desires as a supernatural part of your character and you will be empowered by His Spirit to live the life He desires for you.

Each day your devotional will provide:
- Focused Scripture Passage
- Devotional Reading
- Personal Reflection Questions
- Today's Prayer
- Statement of Being

Join me on this 30-day journey to writing your new story of being who God has created you to be.

Let the journey begin . . .

WEEK 1

Day 1
Being Accepted

Day 2
Being Blessed

Day 3
Being Chosen

Day 4
Being Dependent (Part 1)

Day 5
Being Dependent (Part 2)

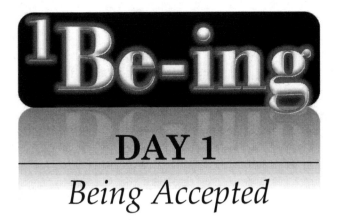

DAY 1

Being Accepted

Main Entry: ¹ac·cept·ed
Pronunciation: \ik- 'sept əd\
Function: *adjective*
Definition: generally approved

"Accept one another, then, just as Christ accepted you, in order to bring praise to God." (Romans 15:7)

BEING ACCEPTED IS THE STATE OF BEING ONE WHO IS accepted by God. Throughout the Bible, the word *accepted* is often associated with the ability to *be accepted* by God. In the Old Testament, the way that people were accepted by God was by offering Him an unblemished sacrifice designed to cover their sins so that they would be acceptable in God's presence. When the proper sacrifice was made, God accepted the offering and subsequently accepted the person that offered the sacrifice. In the New Testament, those of us who have accepted the sacrifice of Jesus' life for our sins have the benefit of being accepted because of the proper sacrifice that He has been made for us through Jesus.

Jesus lived a perfect life on earth. He died on the cross as the sacrifice for our sins. He was buried in a grave confirming His death, rose from the dead and appeared to over 500 people demonstrating His power to forgive. He gave us victory over sin and eternal death. If you put your faith in Christ's sacrifice for your life, you will be saved from the sins of your past, present, and future and be fully accepted into the family of God forever. You will be approved of by God – not because of the good things you do – but because of the perfect work that Christ has done.

Being accepted by God through the sacrifice of Christ, releases us to accept others as they are, as we have been accepted by the God of all creation. Often, when we do not feel accepted, we reject others to feel better about ourselves. Cain struggled with this challenge in the Old Testament. Cain's brother, Abel, offered God a better sacrifice and Cain rejected Abel so much, he killed him because his offering was accepted by God. God responded to his sin by saying:

> "If you do what is right, will you not be accepted? But if you do not do what is right, sin is crouching at your door; it desires to have you, but you must rule over it." (Genesis 4:7)

You will be accepted today by doing the only thing you can do to be right with God: accept the sacrifice of His son, Jesus, for your sins by inviting Him into your life to be your forgiver and leader. You can do this by praying this simple prayer:

God, I acknowledge that I am a sinner and I have broken your law deserving death and punishment, but today I accept the sacrifice of your son Jesus for my sins. I believe that He died on the cross for my sins and rose from the dead to give me new life. Jesus, I am asking you to come into my life. Change me. Transform me. Renew me. Make

18

DAY 1 [1]be-ing

me a new creation. Be my savior and my leader, in Jesus' name. Amen.

If you have already accepted Christ as your Savior, pray this prayer:

Lord, I have not accessed all of the benefits that you made available to me by dying on the cross. The issue of acceptance was settled when I accepted you as my savior, as I was accepted by your Father. Help me to live today, knowing that you accept me even when others choose not to, as your acceptance is what is most important in life.

Statement of Being: Today, I will choose to be accepted because God has accepted me into his family!

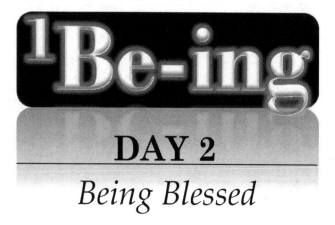

DAY 2

Being Blessed

Main Entry: ¹bless·ed
Pronunciation: \ 'ble-səd \
Function: *adjective*
Definition: bringing pleasure, contentment, or good fortune; enjoying the bliss of heaven

God blessed them and said to them, "Be fruitful and increase in number; fill the earth and subdue it. Rule over the fish in the sea and the birds in the sky and over every living creature that moves on the ground." (Genesis 1:28)

BEING BLESSED IS THE STATE OF BEING SOMEONE WHO BRINGS pleasure to God, is content and experiences good fortune. It is enjoying the bliss of heaven. God wants you to experience a glimpse of heaven while you are here on earth. Jesus says the thief comes to steal, kill and destroy, but I come that you may have life, and have it to the full. He wants to give you a life that is full of joy and contentment. So how does that happen? What does it look like to be blessed?

Being blessed means that you are being fruitful. God is watering the ground of your life so that it produces life in others; that is the command God gave Adam and Eve as they awoke in the Garden of Eden . . . to be fruitful. Each day God invites us to partner with Him in being fruitful, through allowing our life to bring life to others through a kind word or a meaningful look. Today, when you go to the grocery store, try being a blessing by greeting the cashier, looking them in the eyes and asking, "How are you today?" Then wait to listen for what their day has been like, as they scan the items you have purchased. Or I invite you to go visit someone in a hospital or a nursing home and invite them to share their story with you. You will notice that you are being blessed by being a blessing. You will be encouraged as you have sought to encourage someone else. This will be a mutually edifying experience between you and the person that you have sought to bless.

Being blessed also means that you are conquering challenges in your life. That is what it means to subdue; to overcome challenges that present themselves in your life. Blessed people are not void of challenges, but through the power of Christ they are able to overcome challenges that arise in their lives. In Romans 8:37 Paul teaches us that, *"in all things we are more than conquerors through him who loved us."*

Through Christ, who loved us, we can conquer the challenge of fear or failure, because we know we are loved. In 1 John 4:18, John reminds us, *"There is no fear in love. But perfect love drives out fear, because fear has to do with punishment. The one who fears is not made perfect [complete] in love."* When we realize that we are not going to be punished by God if we fail, we can live life free from the fear of failure. Through the love of Christ, we can conquer the challenge of pride or pain, because we realize that our salvation is by grace, and that God will give us grace to endure the pain that comes in our life. We can conquer the challenge of disappointment or depression, because Christ loves us and He died to heal us from all our diseases. We can conquer anything that comes in life because Christ loves us fully.

Being blessed is the privilege of being fruitful, as well as being a conqueror through Him who loved us so that we can be a blessing to others. Can you imagine how much you could bless the people in your world when you commit to being fruitful and when you are conquering challenges in your own life? People will be drawn to the power of Christ in your life and seek to be blessed as you are blessed.

Personal Reflection Questions:

1. Reflect on the people in your life who you would consider to be blessed. What sets them apart from other people in your life?

2. Prior to reading today's devotional how would you have defined being blessed? How has your view of being blessed changed today?

3. Write down one way that you plan to be a blessing to someone else today.

DAY 2 [1]be-ing

Today's Prayer: *Lord, I want to live a blessed life that brings you pleasure, where I experience contentment and good fortune. I want to have a glimpse of heaven on earth so I pray your will be done on earth as it is in heaven. Help me to be a blessing to others today, so through me you can water the ground of their life to produce life in others. Help me to conquer any challenges I experience today without the fear of failure or punishment knowing that I am loved by you.*

Statement of Being: Today, I choose to be blessed because Christ has fully loved me!

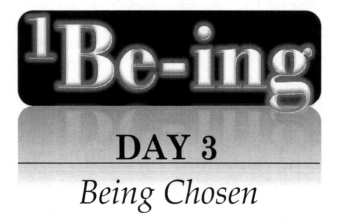

DAY 3

Being Chosen

Entry: ¹cho·sen
Pronunciation: \ˈchō-zᵊn\
Function: *adjective*
Definition: elected, carefully selected, selected or marked for favor or special privilege

The LORD said to Samuel, "How long will you mourn for Saul, since I have rejected him as king over Israel? Fill your horn with oil and be on your way; I am sending you to Jesse of Bethlehem. I have chosen one of his sons to be king."(1 Samuel 16:1)

BEING CHOSEN IS THE STATE OF BEING ONE THAT HAS BEEN elected and carefully selected, or marked for favor, or special privilege. King David's life is a beautiful picture of being chosen because he lived as if he was chosen by God before his election was official. God was working in David's life and the life of those around him to affirm that he was the king.

24

In 1 Samuel 16, we see characteristics of someone that is being chosen.

GOD CHOOSES PEOPLE WHO ARE CONSECRATED

God told the prophet Samuel to have David's family consecrate themselves to prepare a sacrifice to the Lord. Consecration is the process of being set apart for something special. David's family was being consecrated while he was away taking care of the sheep. God wanted the family consecrated before the new king was revealed to them. The family needed to be consecrated, but only David was already consecrated. He had already been set aside by God to be the king of Israel. In order to be a person that is chosen by God, you have to be willing to be consecrated and set aside for his use. God wants to use every gift and ability that He has given you for his glory, but He cannot do that without a consecrated person. Being chosen involves you choosing to consecrate yourself before the Lord.

GOD CHOOSES PEOPLE WHO HAVE CHARACTER

David was the youngest of eight brothers. In his time, being the youngest sibling disqualified you for expected leadership. When Samuel came to Jesse's house, he assumed that the king must be one of the older brothers who looked, walked, spoke, and even smelled like a king. But God shared a distinguishing characteristic with Samuel that allowed him to see David as the king that God had chosen him to be. God told Samuel that He does not look at the outward appearance, but He looks at the heart. God looks at the motives and intentions of our heart. David was chosen because he had the character to be king. God focused on his heart instead of his height or handsomeness. David's character allowed him to watch the sheep when no one was watching him. Who are you when no one is looking? Are

25

you a person of your word? When you think about your desire to reach goals in life, are you more focused on developing your heart or your outward appearance? Do you spend more time getting ready for work, or for a date than you do connecting with God on a daily basis? God chooses people of character, knowing that your gifts may elevate you to a position of honor, or respect, but your character will keep you there.

GOD CHOOSES PEOPLE WHO ARE CONSISTENT

David was chosen by God because he was consistent. Day in and day out, he consistently cared for the sheep. When Samuel asked Jesse if he had any other sons, Jesse was able to answer with confidence that David, his youngest son, was watching the sheep. He knew where to find David because David consistently did what he was supposed to do. David consistently cared for the sheep, instead of choosing to play with the insects or play with his friends. David consistently cared for the sheep even when they were threatened by lions and bears. His consistency in caring for sheep prepared him to care for God's people as the King of Israel. Being chosen involves being consistent.

All of us are chosen to be something. Maybe you have been chosen to be a parent because God trusts you with a child. Maybe you have been chosen to be a leader because God wants to use your gifts to influence others. Maybe you have been chosen to be a friend to a person in a time of need because God knows that you can comfort and encourage them best in this season of life. Whatever God has chosen you to be, I challenge you to be confident in being his choice. God does not make mistakes. If He chose you, He will prepare you to fulfill the purpose for which He chose you.

DAY 3 [1]be-ing

<u>Personal Reflection Questions:</u>

1. Write down at least one area of your personal life that needs to be consecrated and set apart for God.

2. Our culture focuses so much on the outward appearance, that often we, like Samuel, confuse attractiveness with trustworthiness. Reflect on a time when you have been more focused on the outward appearance, instead of the heart? What is one area of your character in which you would like to experience growth during this season of your life?

3. All of us are consistent at something. Name one area where you are naturally consistent. In what area of your life would you like to be more consistent?

Today's Prayer: *Lord, I thank you that you have chosen me to do something unique in this world. You have a purpose for my life that is only for me. Help me to live today as if I am chosen, because I am. I want to be consecrated for your purposes. I want to be a person of character with a heart that is pure before you. I want to be consistent in my daily choices so when you look for me, you will know where to find me. Like David, I will be doing what my Father has asked. Help me to live a chosen life today.*

Statement of Being: Today, I will choose to be chosen because God has chosen me for such a time as this!

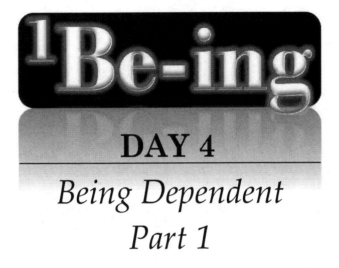

DAY 4

Being Dependent
Part 1

Main Entry: ¹de·pen·dent
Pronunciation: \di-'pen-dənt\
Function: *adjective*
Definition: relying on another for support

"I am the vine; you are the branches. If a man remains in me and I in him, he will bear much fruit; apart from me you can do nothing."
(John 15:6)

BEING DEPENDENT IS THE STATE RELYING ON ANOTHER FOR support. When a baby is born to a mother and a father, the baby steps into a world in which they are completely dependent upon their parents. A baby cannot feed, clothe or clean itself. A baby cannot walk or talk. If a baby tried to feed, clothe or clean itself, the parents would be surprised. If the baby started to walk or talk right out the womb, the parents would be in shock! As a baby enters the world, it enters a new state of the United States, the STATE OF DEPENDENCE!

As the baby grows older, the baby begins to learn more skills that allow them to become less dependent upon the parents. A baby grows from holding a bottle to using utensils, from crawling to walking, from babbling to talking. By the time a baby is three years-old, their favorite word is "MINE." A baby has not worked for food, clothes or toys, but as a part of human nature, a baby begins to desire independence and personal ownership.

After a few more years, a baby grows from being a toddler to a child, from a child to an adolescent, and from an adolescent to an adult . . . all the while growing more and more independent from their parents. Finally, the parents can no longer claim the child as a dependant on their income taxes, as the parents no longer provide most of their child's daily needs.

Today, as you reflect on Jesus' words to his disciples, ask yourself, "Can God still claim you as a dependant on His taxes?" As you have grown spiritually, have you adopted a July 4th mentality to the spiritual life, living as if each day was Independence Day? Our lack of dependence on God does not happen overnight. Like a child, it starts with gaining skills, knowledge and even some level of proficiency, until ultimately we begin to live our lives without God's direction or assistance. We only come to him in emergency room situations when we need to take advantage of His insurance card signed with grace and mercy.

Being dependent involves choosing to . . .

REMAINED CONNECTED

Jesus describes Himself as the vine and his disciples as the branches that need to remain connected in order to bear fruit. He tells them that apart from Him they can do nothing. Jesus did not mean that apart from Him they could not wake up, wash clothes, eat food or walk to the market. He was really emphasizing the fact that apart from Him they could not do anything of spiritual value or lasting significance. In order to produce spiritual fruit, they had to stay connected to Jesus.

We remain connected through prayer. Prayer is inviting God into our business. God wants to be consulted on everything related to our day. We can add habits to our lives to assure that we are praying continually. We can pray before every meeting. We can pray during the normal meal times of the day. We can choose to pray while we are sitting in traffic. The key is to remain continually available to God. Continual prayer keeps us from having "No God" zones. Are you praying like you need God? See 1 Thessalonians 5:17.

We also remain connected through Bible study. Bible study is integrating God's opinion into our daily lives. When we study the Bible, God teaches us what we have yet to learn. God rebukes us and lets us know when we are wrong. He also corrects us so that we can get back on track and then He trains us so that we can be prepared for everything that He has called us to do. Do you study Scripture as if you need God? See 2 Timothy 3:16-17.

We also remain connected through worship. Worship is intimacy with God. When we worship God, we can more clearly see His heart and His desires. When we worship God, He reveals more of our heart and desires to us. In John 4:24, Jesus says that true worshippers must worship God in spirit and in truth. Worshipping Him in spirit allows us to worship Him out of our spirit, not out of our flesh. We can only worship Him from the inside out. Worshipping Him in truth means that we worship Him based on the truth we have come to know about Him through our personal relationship. When He saved us from our sins, we started worshipping Him as our forgiver and redeemer. When He provided our needs, we started worshipping Him as our provider. When He healed our bodies, we started worshipping Him as our healer. Do you worship as if you need God?

Anytime we think that we do not need to pray because we know enough to do it on our own, we are not being dependent. Anytime we think that we can make a decision based on what makes sense, instead of what is written in Scripture, we are not being dependent. Anytime we think that we can know the heart of God without seeking His face through worship, we are not being dependent. When we subtly declare independence from God, we begin to see our spiritual fruit dying on the vine.

The best way for me to remember that I need to remain connected to Christ is to remember how dependent I am on my visual aids. I have worn glasses or contacts for most of my life. I would never leave the house and try to do a days' worth of work without my glasses because without them my vision is not clear. I would never drive onto the freeway without my glasses because I could have an accident and injure myself or someone else. Similarly, when we do not stay connected to Christ through prayer, Bible study and worship, we find ourselves having accidents that injure ourselves and those close to us. We find ourselves tripping up and saying things we wish we had not said. Being dependent requires that we remain connected to Christ.

Personal Reflection Questions:

1. Which area of remaining connected is God challenging you to grow in this week . . . Prayer, Bible Study or Worship?

2. How do you plan to incorporate prayer and worship into your daily experience so that God can be invited into the intimate details of your life?

3. In which role do you feel God is using your Bible Study time to develop you . . . teaching, rebuking, correcting or training? Explain.

Today's Prayer: *Lord, I want to depend on you, but often I just get caught in the daily routine of going through life without inviting you into my business, integrating your opinion or intimately connecting with you in worship. Today I pray that I would intentionally depend on you as I live the life that you have given me. Remind me today of my need for you and your availability to me. Thank you for being someone I can depend on.*

Statement of Being: Today, I will choose to depend on God even when it does not seem like I need to.

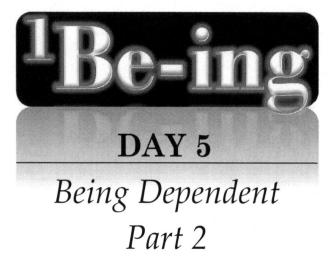

DAY 5

Being Dependent
Part 2

A S WE GROW IN OUR FAITH BY LEARNING TO DEPEND ON God as our Father, we realize that we are walking in a personal relationship with Him that is dynamic and interactive. Our connection to our heavenly Father is not just one that is based in doing our chores (ministry), but in being His children. Since we are God's children, let us continue learning to be dependent on Him today.

Being dependent on God involves choosing to . . .

REFRAME THE CONNECTION

"You are my friends if you do what I command. ¹⁵ I no longer call you servants, because a servant does not know his master's business. Instead, I have called you friends, for everything that I learned from my Father I have made known to you." (John 15:14-15)

Being dependent requires us to reframe the connection we have with Christ so that we keep the passion in our relationship with Him. It is one thing to remain connected through prayer, Bible study, and worship because we feel that we have to. It is another thing to remain connected because we want to. I am not saying that our relationship with God should be based solely on our desire, because our desires may change. Sometimes, we will not feel like inviting God into our business, integrating his opinion or being intimate through worship, but we demonstrate our love for Him not just through our desires, but through our discipline. We demonstrate our love through more than the power of our feelings but through the power of our choice. That is true love!

As a husband, there are times that I do not feel like demonstrating love, but true love allows me to move beyond my feelings to make the choice to love. Similarly, Jesus wants us to choose to love Him by doing what He commands, making us friends, not servants. Sometimes, we need to remember that we are not only servants of God, but first we are children of God. God loves us because of who we are to Him (His children), not because of what we do for Him (as His servants). Servants have to serve their master. Friends choose to serve their friends.

REMEMBER HIS COMMITMENT

"You did not choose me, but I chose you and appointed you to go and bear fruit--fruit that will last. Then the Father will give you whatever you ask in my name." (John 15:16)

Being dependent requires us to remember His commitment to us. We can depend on God because He initiated the relationship before we chose to respond. Romans 5:8 says, *"But God demonstrates his own love for us in this: While we were still sinners, Christ died for us."* God chose us, appointed us, and provided everything that we needed to be effective in making His name great. God did all of this, knowing everything about us, so we can depend on Him.

When I was in high school, my father promised me that he would give me the money I needed to buy lunch every day at school. Even when I would not finish washing dishes or folding the clothes, my lunch money was connected to his commitment, not my performance. The more he kept his commitment, the more I knew I could depend on him to provide what I needed. Likewise, the more we see God doing what He has committed to do – choosing us, appointing us, and providing for us – the more we can trust and depend on Him.

Personal Reflection Questions

1. Think about your connection with Christ: do you see yourself as God's child, or as His servant? Explain.

2. Reflect on how God has demonstrated His commitment to you in a season when you did not keep your commitment to Him. How has that changed the way you relate to God?

Today's Prayer: *God, I remember what it was like to depend on you, as a child depends on a parent. During the rough times in my life, I have called on you and you have been there for me, while at other times I have lived as if you were not there. Help me to be more mindful of my dependence on you. I realize that without you I cannot do anything that will last beyond me. Help me depend on you today. Remind me to remain connected to you throughout the day. Help me to reframe my connection with you so I can live as your child and not just your servant. Thank you for keeping your commitment to me even when I have failed to keep all of my commitments to you. I love you.*

Statement of Being: Today, I will choose to be dependent on God as His child and not just His servant.

WEEK 2

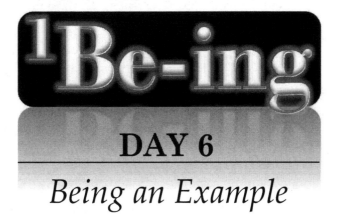

DAY 6

Being an Example

Main Entry: ¹ex·am·ple
Pronunciation: \ig-'zam-pəl\
Function: *noun*
Definition: one that serves as a pattern to be imitated or not to be imitated

Follow my example, as I follow the example of Christ.
(1 Corinthians 12:1)

BEING AN EXAMPLE IS THE STATE OF BEING ONE WHO SERVES as a pattern to be imitated by someone else. While in college, I was friends with a young lady who studied fashion design. Intrigued by her craft and the process of moving a dress from conception to design, she taught me something that I have never forgotten. Initially, she spent a significant amount of time developing the dress, sketching the original concept on a piece of paper and then reviewing it. She moved from sketching to drawing and from drawing to designing the dress. As she designed the dress, she always had someone in mind. She imagined how the dress would fit on

41

each part of the body. She visualized how the dress would flow from top to bottom. After a great deal of time outlining the dress, she would finally purchase the material and create a pattern. The pattern provided the parameters and boundaries needed to cut the cloth exactly according to design. In time, this pattern could be used by anyone in the world as an example.

Equally, God has offered us the best pattern of life that can be lived. He gave us the model of Jesus Christ, His one and only son. Jesus lived His life being the pattern of what it looks like to love God and love people. Jesus spent time in private talking to God and He spent time in public caring for the needs of others. Jesus listened with attentiveness to those that society described as invisible and He healed people who were plagued by illness. Jesus was a perfect pattern; having experienced everything we go through, yet doing it without sinning.

After washing His disciples' feet, Jesus told them, "Go and do likewise." After His death and resurrection, He commanded us to go and make disciples of all nations, baptizing them in the name of the Father, the Son, and the Holy Spirit and teaching them to obey everything that He commanded them to do. He promised He would be with us until the end of the age. Jesus was the perfect example for us and He challenged us to imitate His pattern.

Not long after this message was communicated to the disciples, a persecutor named, Saul, was knocked off his animal by a blinding light and Christ transformed him into the greatest missionary of the New Testament known as Paul. Paul wrote two-thirds of the New Testament and spread the gospel throughout the known world. He challenged the church at Corinth to follow his example as he followed the example of Christ. He was reproducing the pattern that was created by the original designer, God. Paul spent his life being such an example that he could encourage others to pattern their lives after his. He was a man of purpose and unwavering focus. No matter what challenges he encountered as a follower of Christ in the first century, he continued to persevere, spending his life making disciples.

You were created by the original designer, based on a pattern that requires an innate desire for a deep connection with Christ and a deep connection with others, as you were created in His image and that is His heart's desire. The pattern continues. You were created to be an example for someone else. Is your life one that is worth imitating? Do you live as if someone is looking up to you? You should because someone is looking up to you as a pattern. If you are an older sibling, your younger siblings are looking up to you. If you are a parent, your children are looking up to you. People at your job are looking up to you and people in your community are looking at your life as an example to either mold themselves after, or to choose the opposite pattern.

After my wife and I were married, we moved into our first home. We prayed that we would have an influence on our community for Christ. We were living such hectic lives that we rarely were able to spend as much time with our neighbors as we desired. We would come home late from a meeting at church or studying for seminary and find our neighbors sitting on the porch hanging out. We prayed that God would give us the ability to balance our lives so we could spend time with them and also enable us to inspire them to spark a relationship with Christ. Occasionally, we would have a conversation on the front lawn, or invite a couple over for dinner, but direct interaction was limited.

After nearly five years, we were preparing to move out of our home. Our neighbor stood on our lawn with tears in his eyes and said, "I am not ready for you all to leave. I have been watching how you love each other and have pursued the purpose you believe God has for you. I have a lot of shortcomings and struggles, but I have been encouraged by your example. I want you to know that three weeks ago, I went to church for the first time in years. Thank you for being a model for what it looks like to love Jesus and love one another." As you can imagine, I was in tears because after nearly five years, our prayer was being answered. Though we were not able to have many direct interactions, we were able to be an example for a person who desired to live a full life in his relationship with God and others. I encourage you to be positive example for someone in your world because they are watching whether you know it, or not.

Personal Reflection Questions

1. Other than Christ, who is the person that has had the greatest impact on your life? How have you been inspired by their example?

2. Who is one person in your world that you realize is looking to you as an example? What steps are taking to be a positive example for them?

3. When you think about the example that Christ left for us, what do you feel He is calling you to do to continue as a pattern of the original designer?

Today's Prayer: *Jesus, thank you for being the greatest example anyone could have. You have been a wonderful big brother in modeling how I am supposed to live my life by loving God and loving others. Teach me to follow your example and to be an example for others. Help me to be aware of those that I currently impact and help me feel empowered to be a positive example. Thank you for the influence you have given me in the lives of my friends and family members. Help me to use my influence to advance your kingdom.*

Statement of Being: Today, I will choose to be a positive example to _____ because they are watching me.

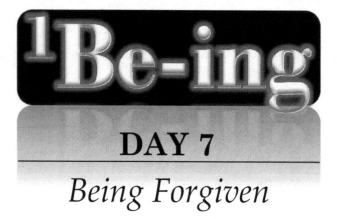

DAY 7

Being Forgiven

Main Entry: ¹for·giv·en
Pronunciation: \ fór-'gi-vən \
Function: *verb*
Definition: to have been granted relief from payment of or to have been forgiven of a debt

Read (Matthew 18:21-35)

²¹ *Then Peter came to Jesus and asked, "Lord, how many times shall I forgive my brother when he sins against me? Up to seven times?"*

²² *Jesus answered, "I tell you, not seven times, but seventy-seven times.*

²³ *"Therefore, the kingdom of heaven is like a king who wanted to settle accounts with his servants.* ²⁴ *As he began the settlement, a man who owed him ten thousand talents was brought to him.* ²⁵ *Since he was not able to pay, the master ordered that he and his wife and his children and all that he had be sold to repay the debt.*

[26] *"The servant fell on his knees before him. 'Be patient with me,' he begged, 'and I will pay back everything.'* [27] *The servant's master took pity on him, canceled the debt and let him go.*

[28] *"But when that servant went out, he found one of his fellow servants who owed him a hundred denarii. He grabbed him and began to choke him. 'Pay back what you owe me!' he demanded.*

[29] *"His fellow servant fell to his knees and begged him, 'Be patient with me, and I will pay you back.'*

[30] *"But he refused. Instead, he went off and had the man thrown into prison until he could pay the debt.* [31] *When the other servants saw what had happened, they were greatly distressed and went and told their master everything that had happened.*

[32] *"Then the master called the servant in. 'You wicked servant,' he said, 'I canceled all that debt of yours because you begged me to.* [33] *Shouldn't you have had mercy on your fellow servant just as I had on you?'* [34] *In anger his master turned him over to the jailers to be tortured, until he should pay back all he owed.*

[35] *"This is how my heavenly Father will treat each of you unless you forgive your brother from your heart."*

BEING FORGIVEN IS THE STATE OF BEING ONE WHO HAS BEEN granted relief from payment of a debt. In our society, debt is a normal part of life. Most individuals buy items using debt with the hope of paying it off later. We commit to making payments for thirty years on a home, ten to twenty years on a school loan, and four to five years on a vehicle – not to mention the items that we purchase for our homes that may take two to three years to pay for, like a refrigerator, furniture and a plasma television. Take some time to consider all of the debt that you owe, from your mortgage lender to your personal credit cards. If you are like most Americans, you probably have more debt than you desire. How would you respond if all of your creditors were to send you a letter in the mail today, communicating that all of your debts were completely paid and you no longer owe anyone any money?

I can see the smile on your face right now. I can feel the sense of joy, relief and excitement. I can feel the sense of sincere appreciation and gratitude. You are feeling the same feeling you should feel daily when you recognize what Christ has done for you. You created the debt through personal choices that were detrimental to your financial future, you knew you were accruing debt, and you planned to pay for it through your own hard work and effort over time. You deserved to pay the debt in full with interest, but someone paid the debt for you. The same is true with our spiritual lives. All of us created debt through paying for sin on credit. We tried to cover all of our sins, but our credit was not extensive enough to cover the debt. We planned to pay for mistakes through our own hard work and effort over time. The Bible says that we all have sinned and fall short of God's glory. The payment for sin is death; therefore we deserve to die physically and spiritually.

Today, I am sending you a letter to let you know that if you have accepted the sacrifice of Jesus Christ on the cross for your sins, your debt has been forgiven. You no longer have to worry about being in debt ever again. You have been *forgiven*. I know you do not deserve it, but you have been forgiven by the only one who could forgive the debt that you owed, Jesus Christ. He lived a perfect life and paid for your debt on the cross. I am here to say with a clear conscious that I am not perfect. In no way would I sit here fooling myself to live as if I am, because I am not. *I am not perfect, but I am forgiven* and that is what gives me confidence to be who God created me to be. I do not have to live as if I have spiritual debt on my books; my debts have been paid.

Now that I know what it feels like to be forgiven, I have an opportunity and an obligation to forgive as Christ has forgiven me. Of course, I have been offended, hurt and disappointed by others. I have the right to remain angry and bitter because currently someone owes me money that has yet to be repaid. Today, someone has hurt my feelings and has not asked for forgiveness. Today, someone has misunderstood me and assumed something that was not true. I have the right to be angry and bitter, but so does Christ. However, He forgave me so that I can choose to follow His example by forgiving others. When we choose not to forgive, we feel the effects of someone else's debt through anger and bitterness. The person that has offended you has moved on, though you are the one feeling the pain and pressure as result. So, I challenge you today to forgive them as Christ has forgiven you, beyond what you deserve or expected, and allow the power of forgiveness to lead you to freedom.

Personal Reflection Questions

1. Reflect on a time when someone forgave you when you did not deserve it. How does that change the way you experience and give forgiveness?

2. For what has God forgiven you that you have yet to accept His forgiveness?

3. Who is a person that you need to forgive as Christ has forgiven you? What is one step you can take to begin forgiving today?

Today's Prayer: *God, thank you for sending your son Jesus to die for me so I could be forgiven of my sins. Thank you for demonstrating your love through the priceless sacrifice you made in allowing your son to die before I chose to follow Him. I know that I did not deserve this, but I receive it freely today. Help me to be consistent in confessing my sins and asking for forgiveness when I sin against you and others. I pray that you will help me to forgive others and myself, as you have forgiven me, and to grant others forgiveness, as well. I want to experience the freedom that you have made available to me by being forgiven, instead of living in the chains of unforgiveness.*

Statement of Being: Today, I will choose to be forgiven because Christ has paid all of my sin debts and released me from the penalty of sin.

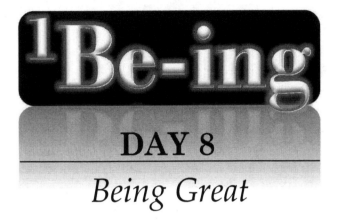

DAY 8

Being Great

Main Entry: ¹great
Pronunciation: \ 'grāt \
Function: *adjective*
Definition: notably large in size, chief or preeminent over others

¹ At that time the disciples came to Jesus and asked, "Who is the greatest in the kingdom of heaven?" ² He called a little child and had him stand among them. ³ And he said: "I tell you the truth, unless you change and become like little children, you will never enter the kingdom of heaven. ⁴ Therefore, whoever humbles himself like this child is the greatest in the kingdom of heaven. (Matthew 18:1-4)

BEING GREAT IS THE STATE OF BEING ONE WHOSE LIFE IS large rising above others. It is interesting that when Jesus was asked to describe the greatest in the kingdom, He described the smallest people in our world, children. He taught the disciples with an illustration they would never forget, a child. He wanted them to get the image so He asked a child to come stand next to him. Picture this . . . the disciples standing tall in stature, believing they have asked a great question. It is likely that prior to the conversation they did not even notice that children were there. The disciples had their eyes focused on Jesus thinking His response would be that the greatest in the kingdom was one of them. Perhaps they looked up expecting Him to speak of Moses or Elijah, who were great in the past. After speculation, Jesus asked them to look down at this little child and as He described greatness.

I can imagine their thought process: "What is so great about a child? They cannot help us rule in the new kingdom that Jesus will bring. They cannot work for a living, or contribute to the treasury. They do not have much to offer. What is so great about a child?" Jesus continues by saying that unless they become like little children, they will never enter the kingdom of heaven. What's so great about a child? Jesus says a child is humble and that is what makes them great.

People who think they are great rarely are. Greatness is not based in making oneself notably large or chief among others; rather it is based in humility. Being great is the byproduct of being humble. James 4:10 says, *"Humble yourselves before the Lord, and he will lift you up."* Humility is choosing not to lift yourself up, but allowing the Lord to do it as you humble yourself before Him.

To truly embrace the greatness that comes from being humble, you have to understand what true humility looks like. True humility is not denying who you are, or deflecting compliments authentically given when you have done well. True humility is simply choosing not to be more or less than who you really are. Children own the fact that they are children. A child is not a baby or an adult; a child is a child. Their humility allows them to ask questions about life when they do not understand. Their humility allows them to let their parents provide what they need. Their humility allows them the freedom to play and enjoy life; to laugh out loud and see the world through simplified eyes.

Children have a pure heart that is often easily wronged, yet easily forgiven. Have you ever heard a child come home from school and say, "John is not my friend anymore because he wouldn't play with me today"? Then later that day, or early the next morning, the child is playing with John as if nothing ever happened.

Children do not focus on differences as much as adults. Instead of being afraid of someone that is different from them, they are actually interested and intrigued to the point of asking questions to understand the differences. For example, children of different cultures do not focus on the difference in culture as much as they are intrigued by the difference of skin color, face structure or hair texture.

Children have what is described by adults as *childlike faith*. A child will go into the arms of a person they do not know, trusting that they will be fine. A child does not fear the worst. A child expects the best. I noticed this to be true when I visited Universal Studios in Orlando this summer. I was afraid to ride the larger roller coasters because I do not have faith that I will not become sick as a result of the long falls, or die due to a malfunctioning part. As an adult, sometimes I have too much information and prior knowledge to possess the faith I need. That is what Jesus meant by being great through embracing childlike faith when it comes to trusting God.

In order to be great in the kingdom, Jesus is calling us to be humble like a child. The keys to the kingdom of God are available to you because the great people in the kingdom humbly ask questions, are humbly provided for, and are humbly forgiving. The great people in the kingdom are humbly connected to those that are different and have the childlike faith that allows them to humbly follow the true great one, Christ.

Personal Reflection Questions

1. Reflect on a time when as a child you demonstrated childlike faith. Write down what you recall about how you lived life then.

2. How is God calling you to humble yourself in this season of your life?

3. Think of the people in your life who have demonstrated their greatness through humility. Write them a small note today letting them know how great they are in your world because of their humility.

Today's Prayer: *Lord, thank you for showing me what it really means to be great. I realize that being great is not about a title or fame, but about choosing to be like a child. Thank you for showing me that I can be your child and become great in your kingdom. Teach me to humble myself so that I can become the great person that you created me to be.*

Statement of Being: Today, I will choose to be great through humbly being God's child.

DAY 9

Being Hungry
Part 1

Being Hungry
Main Entry: ¹hun·gry
Pronunciation: \ˈhəŋ-grē\
Function: *adjective*
Definition: having a craving or urgent need for food or a specific nutrient

Like newborn babies, crave pure spiritual milk, so that by it you may grow up in your salvation, now that you have tasted that the Lord is good. (1 Peter 2:2)

B EING HUNGRY IS THE STATE OF BEING ONE WHO HAS A craving, or urgent need for something; an intense, urgent, abnormal desire, or longing for something. When babies are born, they develop an intense appetite quickly. Once they have tasted milk, their appetite grows. Babies develop by drinking the milk their mother provides. Once they realize milk provides them with the satisfaction and satiation their bodies needs, they cry when they crave milk. The consequence of receiving milk is physical growth. Their heartbeat becomes stronger, their eyes see more clearly, and their mind cognates better. The baby begins a natural, healthy growth pattern.

The same is true in our relationship with God. When we become new believers, we develop an appetite for the things of God quickly. Once we taste the spiritual milk that comes from God's Word, our appetite grows so we can grow spiritually. But at times, it seems that we do not have the spiritual appetite we need to grow as God would want us to grow. Peter encourages us to crave pure, spiritual milk so that we can grow spiritually. When we crave the spiritual milk, our hearts will beat for God's desires, our eyes will see God's vision, and our minds will be transformed to understand God's plan. It all starts with developing a spiritual appetite.

Developing a spiritual appetite involves . . .

FEEDING YOUR SPIRIT CONSISTENTLY

When you feed your body three times a day, your body desires three meals a day.

You must daily feed your spirit with God's Word so that you develop an appetite for it. When you do not feed your spirit, your appetite for Christ dissipates and you are not as hungry for what you need.

[7]Do not be deceived: God cannot be mocked. A man reaps what he sows. [8] The one who sows to please his sinful nature, from that nature will reap destruction; the one who sows to please the Spirit, from the Spirit will reap eternal life. (Galatians 6:7-8)

Paul teaches us that our hunger is connected to our eating patterns. The part of our lives that we feed the most will have the greatest hunger. If we feed our sinful nature, our desire for sin will increase even more, but if we feed our spiritual nature, our desire for God will increase. There is a direct correlation between our feeding patterns. The more we eat spiritual food, the less we desire to sin, but the more we sin, the less we desire the Spirit's way.

FOLLOWING A HEALTHY SPIRITUAL MEAL PLAN

Our appetite is fueled by the meals we are consistently exposed to.

If we expose ourselves to healthy foods, we develop an appetite for healthy foods, but if we consistently expose ourselves to junk food, we become a junk food junkie.

¹⁶ *Let the word of Christ dwell in you richly as you teach and admonish one another with all wisdom, and as you sing psalms, hymns and spiritual songs with gratitude in your hearts to God. (Colossians 3:16)*

Paul teaches us that our spiritual meal plan should include at least three things. First, we should partake in being taught the Bible by a gifted teacher who can explain God's Word in a way that we can understand. Secondly, we should receive admonishment or godly advice from other believers that help us apply the Word of God to our lives. Finally we should take advantage of the ice cold beverage of godly music which prepares our hearts to receive the spiritual food that comes from the Word of God and godly advice. A balanced spiritual diet will help us develop a healthy spiritual appetite.

FORGETTING YOUR SPIRITUAL PAST

Children that eat vegetables and have a bad experience are less likely to try them again.

Forgetting what is behind and straining toward what is ahead, [14] *I press on toward the goal to win the prize for which God has called me heavenward in Christ Jesus. (Philippians 3:13)*

Paul teaches us that forgetting past experiences will help us to be open to God's prepared meals in the future. To forget does not mean that you no longer remember, but it means you no longer allow the past to hinder you from moving forward towards your future. We have to forget the failures that leave us feeling unmotivated and unworthy. If Paul consistently fed himself the memories of killing hundreds of Christians before coming to Christ, his "main courses" in the New Testament would have never been served. We have to forget the successes that leave us feeling content and complacent. If Paul consistently fed himself "happy meals" of success that his developed churches experienced, he would have never continued to develop new churches where more disciples could grow.

Personal Reflection Questions

1. How consistently do you feed your spirit (once a day, twice a day, etc.)? How do you normally feed your spirit?

58

2. Reflect on a time when you were consistently engaging all components of a healthy spiritual meal plan. What effect did it have on your life?

3. What do you need to forget in order to move forward in your spiritual journey?

Today's Prayer: *God, I want to be hungry for you like I hunger for natural food. I want my life to be unsatisfying without your consistent involvement because I know that only you can fill the God-sized space in my life. I pray that you will help me to be consistent in feeding my spirit so that I will be led by your Spirit and not my sinful nature.*

Statement of Being: Today, I will choose to be hungry for spiritual food so I can grow in my faith.

DAY 10

Being Hungry
Part 2

⁶ *Blessed are those who hunger and thirst for righteousness, for they will be filled. (Matthew 5:6)*

HAVE YOU EVER HUNGERED FOR SOMETHING THAT COULD not seem to be satisfied? Maybe you were hungry for something sweet and could not satisfy your sweet tooth, or maybe you wanted a nice juicy steak, but the steak you ordered at the restaurant was overcooked and left you wanting for more. There are few things more frustrating than having a hunger that cannot be satisfied. An insatiable hunger leads to seeking for something else to fill our hunger void.

Within each of us, lies an innate hunger for something that we alone cannot satisfy. We hunger for the significance and depth that only a meaningful relationship with God can provide. We crave a connection with our Heavenly Father in the same way that a young boy desires a meaningful relationship with his father. At some point in life, we recognize this hunger and without knowing where to find satisfaction, we seek to satiate our desire with something that cannot bring satisfaction. We seek fulfillment in a romantic relationship or a successful career. We seek fulfillment in getting married or having children. We seek fulfillment through buying a larger home or a faster car. Our search to taste the sweetness we long for in life is like having a substitute sweetener, when we actually need the real thing.

In Matthew 5, we peek into one of Jesus' most significant conversations with his disciples as He provides the recipe for a life that will ultimately satisfy. He teaches them that the key to being satisfied is developing a healthy appetite for the right things. Food cannot satisfy the desire for a relationship with the Father. Jesus' promise to His disciples was that if they developed a healthy appetite, they would be filled. Let us continue being hungry for righteousness today.

Being hungry involves . . .

FORGING SPIRITUAL PARTNERSHIPS

Develop friendships with people that eat the same types of things you desire to eat.

Nothing is more frustrating than wanting to eat a healthy balance of foods, while being close to someone who does not care about your interest in healthy eating. You try to watch your calorie intake, while at dinner they eat a large appetizer, a larger main course, and the largest desert. Similarly, when we have an acute appetite for the things of God, we need others around us who can help us stick to our spiritual diet.

"As iron sharpens iron, so one man sharpens another."
(Proverbs 27:17)

Solomon teaches us that our appetite for spiritual food will be sharper as we surround ourselves with people who are spiritually hungry as well.

Do not be misled: "Bad company corrupts good character."
(1 Corinthians 15:33)

Paul teaches us that our good intentions to eat spiritually healthy meals can be compromised by friends who do not have a similar appetite. Surrounding yourself with spiritually fit people will help your figure begin to take shape.

FILLING YOUR SPIRITUAL STOMACH
When you fill yourself with healthy food, there is little room for unhealthy substitutions.

Blessed are those who hunger and thirst for righteousness, for they will be filled. (Matthew 5:6)

Jesus promises that we will be blessed when we are hungry for righteousness, and our desire will be filled by our Father who provides all that we need.

Do not get drunk on wine, which leads to debauchery. Instead, be filled with the Spirit. (Ephesians 5:18)

Paul teaches us that when filled with the Spirit, we have less of a desire to become inebriated on spirits and shots, because the boldness, confidence, and freedom that being drunk provides can come from being filled with the Spirit.

So I say, live by the Spirit, and you will not gratify the desires of the sinful nature. [17] For the sinful nature desires what is contrary to the Spirit, and the Spirit what is contrary to the sinful nature. They are in conflict with each other, so that you do not do what you want. [18] But if you are led by the Spirit, you are not under law. (Galatians 5:16-18)

Paul teaches us that our sinful nature and spiritual nature are in a constant battle with one another. If we want to win the fight, we must invest in the proper feeding program. When we allow our lives to be filled with the Spirit, we will have less and less of an appetite for sinful things.

FOOD FOR THOUGHT

A couple of years ago while on an African Safari, I came deathly close to wild animals. I was not afraid of being eaten by the elephants, zebras, or giraffes, because all of these animals only have an appetite for plants. In a similar way, when you develop an appetite for the food of the Spirit, you will not feel as tempted to partake in sinful meals that move you further away from God because you will have a strong appetite for growing closer to God.

Personal Reflection Questions:

1. Write down the names of two friends that you need to draw close in your pursuit to being hungry for God. Consider inviting them to join you on this 30-day journey to being who God created you to be.

2. What hunger in your life normally competes with your hunger for God? What steps can you take to make sure your Spirit wins the competition over your sinful nature?

3. Reflect on a time in your life where you were spiritually strong enough to resist unhealthy spiritual food. What helped you develop a healthy appetite for God then?

Today's Prayer: *Lord, I realize that my friends have a lot to do with who I am and who I will become. Help me to seek out spiritual friendships that will support me in my desire to develop a deeper hunger for you. I know that as I hunger for you, I will be filled and I want to enjoy my spiritual meals with others. I pray that you will help me to curb the appetite I have for things that do not please you and allow me to be empowered by your Spirit to walk in your way.*

Statement of Being: Today, I will choose to be hungry through pursuing spiritual partnerships.

WEEK 3

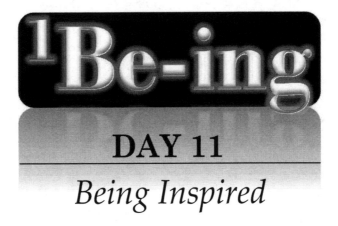

DAY 11

Being Inspired

Main Entry: ¹inspired
Pronunciation: \ in-ˈspī(-ə)rd \
Function: *adjective*
Definition: influenced, moved, or guided by divine or supernatural inspiration

We continually remember before our God and Father your work produced by faith, your labor prompted by love, and your endurance inspired by hope in our Lord Jesus Christ. (1 Thessalonians 1:3)

BEING INSPIRED IS THE STATE OF BEING ONE WHO IS influenced, moved and guided by divine or supernatural inspiration. When you came to Christ, someone inspired you through their words or their life to consider allowing Christ to forgive you of your sins and accept Him as your leader. It may have been a gifted pastor or teacher who God used to share the message of Christ. It may have been a family member or friend who modeled His unconditional love. Whatever the case, you were inspired, influenced, moved or guided by divine or supernatural inspiration to make that life changing choice of accepting Christ's sacrifice.

Now that you know Christ, within you is that same power to be inspired. This word inspire comes from a Latin word that means, *to breathe*. When we are inspired, it is as if we have new levels of breath for the marathon of life. As a student in high school, I ran long distance races of one to three miles per week. During our training sessions, we consistently trained to run over forty-five miles per week. The goal was for us to run beyond our race length so that we gained a greater level of endurance in our muscles and our breathing and the race would therefore be easier. I was one of those runners that began slowly, but my training prepared me to stabilize my breathing during the race, while others were struggling along. No matter how gifted a runner is, when they lose their breath, they always lose the race. No matter how much God has gifted you, if you don't have places in your life where God can breathe into you again, you will not excel or endure in this spiritual journey.

BE INSPIRED BY THE GIFT OF LIFE
". . . the LORD God formed the man from the dust of the ground and breathed into his nostrils the breath of life, and the man became a living being." (Genesis 2:7)

When God created Adam, He separated him from the rest of creation by breathing into his nostrils the breath of life. Animals were breathing air, but Adam was breathing life. This life was not only a life of existence; it was a life of meaning framed in a personal relationship with God. Adam knew God intimately and God knew Adam intimately. Through the divine inspiration that came from the breath of God, Adam was able to fulfill his purpose. He was given the authority to name every animal that was on the earth. Can you imagine how much inspiration it takes to come up with the name for every animal ever created by God? We struggle to come up with a name for our dog or cat, yet Adam was able to name all of the animals with ease because he was inspired through the gift of life from God.

BE INSPIRED BY THE WORD OF LIFE

All Scripture is God-breathed and is useful for teaching, rebuking, correcting and training in righteousness, so that the man of God may be thoroughly equipped for every good work. (2 Timothy 3:16-17)

Every passage in the Bible, from Genesis to Revelation, was inspired *by* God so that you could be inspired *for* God. When the Bible was written, each person wrote inspired by God to deliver a message that would be useful for teaching, rebuking, correcting, and training in righteousness, so we would be sufficiently prepared for all God wants us to do. The reason you and I need to spend time daily in Scripture is because in reading God's Word we receive the breath we need from Him to fulfill His purpose for our lives that day. How can you not be inspired by the story of Moses facing Pharaoh and by God's power to free the Israelites? How can you not be inspired by the story of Joseph who has a dream at seventeen- years-old and walks with God through a series of trials to see that dream come to pass at the age of thirty? How can you not be inspired by the story a young boy named David who killed a giant with one smooth stone and a sling shot? How can you not be inspired by the story of Mary, the mother of Jesus, who trusted the Holy Spirit with her body to give birth to the Savior of the world? God inspired the writers to write words that would breathe inspiration into our lives for each new day.

69

In our opening passage, Paul was inspired by the church at Thessalonica because the church was one that was inspired by hope in the Lord Jesus Christ. This church received life and energy to endure significant struggles through the promise of the Savior. The congregation's hope was fueled by faith that produced work and love that prompted labor. Paul, who wrote two-thirds of the New Testament, was inspired by their hope. Who are you inspiring today? What story in your life can you tell of God's goodness that would inspire (breathe) life into someone else? I know that God has given you life and He has given you His word of life, so I encourage you to be inspired to be an inspiration today.

Personal Reflection Questions

1. Who is the most inspiring person you have encountered? What made them so inspirational?

2. Reflect on a time when someone inspired you and how it affected your life.

3. Who is a person that you can inspire today? How will you choose to inspire that person today?

DAY 11 [1]be-ing

Today's Prayer: *God, I have received inspiration through the breath of life you have given me, but at times I do not feel inspired. Help me to be inspired by the gift and words of life so I can do all that you want me to do. Help me to be an inspiration to others so that I can breathe life into them as you have breathed life into me.*

Statement of Being: Today, I will choose to be inspired because I have received the breath of life.

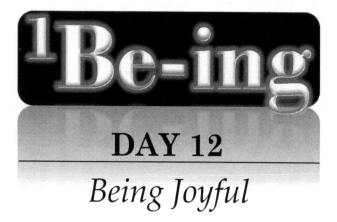

DAY 12

Being Joyful

Main Entry: ¹joy·ful
Pronunciation: \ˈjȯi-fəl\
Function: *adjective*
Definition: describing the emotion evoked by well-being, success, or good fortune or by the prospect of possessing what one desires

Read Psalm 126
¹ *When the LORD brought back the captives to Zion,*
  we were like men who dreamed.
² *Our mouths were filled with laughter,*
  our tongues with songs of joy.
Then it was said among the nations,
  "The LORD has done great things for them."
³ *The LORD has done great things for us,*
  and we are filled with joy.

⁴ *Restore our fortunes, O LORD,*

like streams in the Negev.
⁵ *Those who sow in tears*
    will reap with songs of joy.
⁶ *He who goes out weeping,*
    carrying seed to sow,
will return with songs of joy,
    carrying sheaves with him.

BEING JOYFUL IS THE STATE OF BEING ONE THAT EXPERIENCES the emotion evoked by well-being, success, good fortune, or by the prospect of possessing what one desires. Christ's joy is a unique emotion that we have; the *true* privilege of experiencing delight as believers in Christ. Our joy is different from happiness. Happiness is based in what happens to us, joy is based on the Lord who is for us. Joy allows us to smile in the midst of a storm and have hope in a horrible situation, as we know who is in control.

In Psalm 126, we see the people of God celebrating their freedom from exile and captivity.

JOY IS INCREASED BY SINGING A SONG TO THE LORD

Music is a powerful weapon, used for good, or evil. Some people use music to woo women into vulnerable positions where they can take advantage of their emotions, while others use music to lace a distorted message of life into the mind of a young person. Though music can be used for evil, I believe we can experience the power of music bringing joy to life. All of us have moments in our lives where music has helped us to get through a tough time, or moments where music reminded us of a time when God was there. It might have been a hymn you learned as a child in Sunday School, a new song that you heard on the radio, or in a worship service. Whatever the case, I have

73

learned that singing a song to the Lord can bring joy to your heart when your mind is distressed. Singing a song of praise to the Lord can transform weeping into worshipping. Singing changes our perspective and allows us to see that God is bigger than any problem we may go through.

I encourage all believers to develop their personal "Top 10" list of music that connects them with God. Think about all of the songs that transformed you in the middle of a mess, or that inspired you during a test. Think of all of the songs that drew you closer to Christ, or that allowed you to finally surrender all to his leadership in your life. These songs are songs that can keep the joy level high when the waves of life seem to rise. People will wonder how you can have so much joy in the midst of your situation and you can share your secret weapon of singing praise to the Lord.

JOY IS INCREASED BY RECALLING THE LORD'S GOODNESS

In this passage, the people of God were experiencing a moment of joy, as they were willing to recall the goodness of God bringing them out of exile. When God has freed you from the captivity of sin, you have a reason to be joyful. You can remember what life was like before coming to know Christ and now you know what life is like after coming to know Christ. Sure, things may not be the way that you wish they were, but it is likely that things are not as bad as they *used* to be. God has a way of slowly bringing us to our place of purpose and destiny. He develops faith stories in our lives to remind us of his goodness so that when we come to challenging seasons in life, we can have joy as we recall the goodness God extended to us. This principle was reinforced throughout the Old Testament, as God constantly reminded the people of His deliverance of their forefathers out of the land of Egypt, through the ten plagues, the

Passover, the crossing of the Red Sea and entrance into the promise land.

I encourage all believers to develop a personal list of faith stories that allow you to recall with ease God's goodness in your life. When your joy level is getting low, you can turn to a faith story and be reminded of God's goodness. We all love a great story . . . so much that we will pay over twenty dollars in some cases to buy a story in the form of a movie on DVD. I encourage you to develop a mental movie library of God's goodness so that you can replay it repeatedly during your lifetime. Share your stories with your children and extended family. Exchange stories with your friends, neighbors and co-workers. Impart your story so that God can get the glory and you can have continued joy based on his goodness to you.

I encourage you today to be joyful by singing a song to the Lord and recalling his goodness in your life. No matter how challenging this day may turn out to be, you can choose to be joyful because you know Jesus.

Personal Reflection Questions:

1. What are the top 10 list of songs that you can refer to when you need to increase your joy quotient in life?

    1. _____
    2. _____
    3. _____
    4. _____
    5. _____
    6. _____
    7. _____
    8. _____
    9. _____
   10. _____

2. How would you title three significant faith stories God
    has written in your life?

    1. _____

    2. _____

    3. _____

Today's Prayer: *Lord, I declare today that I will bless you at all times and your praise will always be in my mouth. I am thankful for the ways you have blessed my life. Give me a song to sing and a story to tell of your goodness so that I can be joyful and share that joy with others in my life.*

Statement of Being: Today, I will choose to be joyful because God has been good to me.

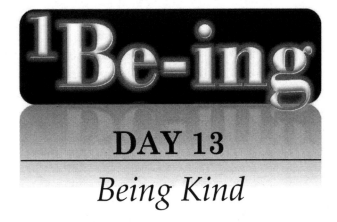

DAY 13

Being Kind

Main Entry: ¹kind
Pronunciation: \ˈkīnd\
Function: *adjective*
Definition: of a sympathetic or helpful nature

. . . love is kind (1 Corinthians 13:4)

BEING KIND IS THE STATE OF BEING ONE WHO IS SYMPATHETIC or helpful in nature. It involves being one who will choose to put themselves in someone else's shoes and ask, "What would I want for someone to do for me?" and then choose to do that for someone else. Have you noticed that this level of kindness is contagious? When we experience kindness, we are more likely to extend kindness to others. This was God's mindset when it came to building a relationship with us. Jeremiah 31:3 reminds us that God drew us to himself through loving-kindness. We draw more to the *love* of God, than the *law* of God. The law often pushes us away, while love draws us closer. Romans 5:8, reminds us that God demonstrated His love

77

for us by allowing Christ to die for us while we were still sinners. Because God is kind and He has made us in His image, being kind is part of being who God created us to be.

I have seen the value of kindness demonstrated profoundly in the life of the church where my wife and I worship and work. The church has ten stated values and one of those values is the value of unnecessary kindness. Our church has strategically chosen to embrace a value of being kind with no strings attached. We have freely passed out over 10,000 bottles of water on the corners of streets in our city and have given thousands of pounds of food away. A few months ago, a woman in our church was suffering from brain cancer and had no personal health insurance. Members of the church decided to host a benefit concert where they raised over $8,000 to assist with her medical bills. This demonstration of unnecessary kindness was impactful to her as well as to all who attended.

I want to encourage you to adopt the value of unnecessary kindness in your personal life by engaging everyone you come across with three forms of kindness:

A KIND LOOK

You can begin being kind by choosing to give a kind look to everyone you engage. Start by looking everyone in the eye when you speak to them and acknowledge their presence with dignity. We live in such a disconnected society that many people do not get a kind look all day long. Whether you are at your job or simply picking up a carton of milk at the grocery store, you can demonstrate kindness through a kind look.

A KIND WORD

You can continue being kind by choosing to share a kind word with everyone you engage. This is one of my favorite parts of being kind; seeking to find something wonderful to say to everyone I meet. For example, you could compliment someone on their smile or their shoes. Everyone has something positive to say about someone, you just have to look for it. You could say, "Hello, how are you today?" and wait for a real response. Kind words are disarming and empowering at the same time. For those who are defensive, kind words begin to break down barriers that hinder them from enjoying meaningful relationships and for those who are open, kind words empower them to be even more open in the future.

A KIND TOUCH

You can continue being kind by choosing to share an appropriate but kind touch to those you come across in a more personal way. A kind touch could be as simple as a handshake or as personal as a hug. Again, since we live in such a disconnected world, many people do not receive a personal touch of any sort all day long. Your demonstration of kindness could provide a level of healing for someone who has been hurt, or you could provide a sense of identification for someone who has been isolated. Obviously, everyone has a different space boundary that they may not feel comfortable with you crossing, but I believe that you can discern that in the moment or simply take the risk and allow them to let you know if they would rather not shake your hand or receive a hug. Men and women will obviously engage this area of kindness differently. Some men will choose to "bump chest" or "fist bump," while some women may feel more comfortable with a hug. Either way, a kind touch combined with a kind word and a kind look will add to the contagious kindness in your world.

When you choose to be kind to your spouse and your children, kindness will saturate your home. When you choose to be kind to your boss and your co-workers, kindness will permeate in your workplace. When you choose to be kind to your neighbors, friends, and even strangers, kindness will envelope your neighborhood. As you choose to be kind, you will begin to see the compound interest of kindness building all around you. A kind environment makes room for Jesus' love to be demonstrated more meaningfully in your life and the lives of others.

Personal Reflection Questions

1. Reflect on a time when someone was kind to you and you particularly noticed their choice to be kind.

2. How does God's kindness motivate you to be kind to others?

3. As you consider sharing a kind look, a kind word and a kind touch, record a couple of ways that you plan to share each of them.

Kind Look	Kind Work	Kind Touch

Today's Prayer: *Lord, I am so thankful for your kindness in my life. You have been kind with no strings attached, so I know You love me. I am asking that You would show me the people and areas in my life where I have not been kind. I want to repent of any unkindness I may have exhibited and ask that You will allow your Spirit to teach me how to be the kind person that You desire in every arena of my life.*

Statement of Being: Today, I will choose to be kind because kindness is contagious.

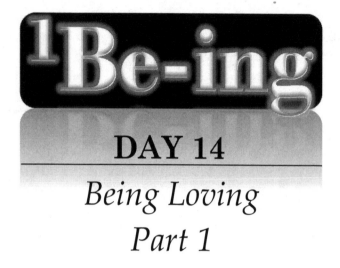

DAY 14

Being Loving
Part 1

Main Entry: ¹lov·ing
Pronunciation: \,lə-viŋ\
Function: *adjective*
Definition: to hold dear, have passion, devotion, or tenderness

He answered: "'Love the Lord your God with all your heart and with all your soul and with all your strength and with all your mind'; and, 'Love your neighbor as yourself.' "(Luke 10:27)

BEING LOVING IS THE STATE OF BEING ONE THAT HOLDS someone else dear, having a passion, devotion or tenderness for them. Being a believer in Christ is rooted in our love for God and our love for others. Jesus told his disciples that they would be known by the way that they loved one another. So, our defining characteristic as a follower of Christ should be love.

In our passage for today, we enter a conversation where Jesus is being tested by a lawyer concerning the law and what it takes to inherit eternal life. Jesus summarizes all Ten Commandments into two brief commandments. We will discuss the first part of the commandment today and the second commandment tomorrow.

The author, Gary Chapman wrote a famous book entitled, *"The Five Love Languages."* In his book, he shares five different ways that we as humans give and receive love. The foundation of his book is that each of us gives and receives love in different languages. So, we may think we are giving love, because we are giving love in our language. But if our spouse or friend receives love in a different language, they have not received the love we thought we gave. In a similar fashion, we may think that we are demonstrating love to God, but we are actually speaking a love language that He does not hear. God wants love in a specific way.

Loving God involves . . .

LOVING GOD WITH ALL YOUR HEART

The heart is the seat of our desires, feelings, affections, and passions. So loving God with all your heart means that God does not want anything, or anyone to have more of your passion than he does. God does not want to play second fiddle to your family, your job, your friendship or your hobbies. To love God with all your heart means to be more passionate about Him than anything else in life.

LOVING GOD WITH ALL YOUR SOUL

The soul is comprised of our psyche, a combination of our spiritual and immortal nature along with its rational and natural faculties, wills, and appetites. The soul is the place where we make our decisions. Decisions may be influenced from the heart, but they are made in the soul. So, to love God with all your soul means to have all of your decisions intimately connected to His will and His desires for your life.

LOVING GOD WITH ALL YOUR STRENGTH

Our strength includes our physical strength and our natural abilities. Loving God with all of your strength requires that you use every one of your abilities to love and serve God. Because God is the Creator and has given you the abilities, He wants exclusive rights to your abilities to use for His glory. Loving God with all of your strength involves surrendering the skills that you have acquired through natural progression, education and experience to Him.

LOVING GOD WITH ALL YOUR MIND

The mind consists of your understanding, intellect, thought processes, operation of reason and manner of thought. Loving God with your mind involves choosing to study God to find out what He wants, and provide it before He asks for it. In Psalm 63 David said that he thought of God while he was preparing to sleep and into the watches of the night. David was thinking about what it would take to please God and trying to do it before being asked for it.

Loving God is at the heart of what it means to be who God has created you to be. We were created for a relationship with God, so learning to love Him according to His way is most important. I encourage you to love God with your heart so that no one person or thing has more of your desire. Love Him with your soul so that your decisions are framed by His purposes. Love God with your strength so that He gets the best of your abilities, not just your job. Love God with your entire mind so that He knows you have been thinking about Him long before He asks you for what He desires from you.

Personal Reflection Questions

1. Which area of loving God seems most natural for who you are? Explain.

2. Which area of loving God seems more challenging for you to engage consistently?

3. How do you plan to love God differently as a result of today's devotional?

Today's Prayer: *God, I do love you. I love you more than I can put into words. I pray that you would teach me how to love you the way you desire to be loved. Help me to put my best into loving you, as you put your best into loving me. I pray that I would intentionally love you will all my heart, soul, strength and mind today.*

Statement of Being: Today, I will choose to *"be loving"* towards God because God is love.

DAY 15

Being Loving
Part 2

He answered: "'Love the Lord your God with all your heart and with all your soul and with all your strength and with all your mind'; and, 'Love your neighbor as yourself.' "(Luke 10:27)

WHILE LOVING GOD WITH ALL OUR HEART, WITH ALL OUR soul, with all our strength and all our mind, God has called us to love our neighbor as ourselves. Today, we are going to continue considering what it means to *"be loving"*. In order to fulfill the greatest commandment, we must be willing to love others as we love ourselves. Many people live on one of the two extremes in this area. Either they will spend most of their time doing what they believe to be best for them while neglecting everyone else, or they will spend most of the their time doing what others want them to do while neglecting themselves. Honestly, you cannot effectively love someone else until you learn to love yourself.

Loving yourself involves . . .

KNOWING YOURSELF

In order to love yourself you have to begin with knowing yourself. Do you know what makes you happy? Do you know what you enjoy doing for fun or for refreshment? Do you know your personality, how it connects to who God has created for you to be, and what He has created you to do? Knowing yourself is what I describe as personal identity development. Through our life experiences we are given opportunities to discover who we are. We have a chance to discover where we have come from and what we value. We have a chance to encounter other people and discover who we are in light of the dissonance we experience in their presence. When God made you, He made you specifically and uniquely. Loving yourself beings with knowing yourself.

ACCEPTING YOURSELF

In order to love yourself well, you must not only know yourself, but you must begin to accept yourself. Have you noticed that many people want to be something or someone that they are not? Individuals with a light skin complexion desire a tan and individuals with a darker complexion often desire to be lighter. People with straight hair want curly hair and people with curly hair want straight hair. People who are tall and thin want to have muscles and curves, while people who are muscular and curvy want to be tall and thin. Why is this? As humans we often struggle to accept ourselves. Our society teaches us to be unique, yet there is something inside us that wants to be like someone else. Accepting yourself involves taking inventory of who you are and distinguishing between the characteristics that can or should be changed from the characteristics that cannot be changed. Accepting yourself means that you accept the things about you that you cannot change. This includes accepting your age, gender, ethnic identity, and core personality. These things are a part of the way God made you for a reason. To love God well, you need to accept them. To love others well, you need to accept it as well because if you have not accepted it, you will find yourself projecting onto others who you feel you are or you will find yourself rejecting others for being who they are.

CELEBRATING YOURSELF

Loving yourself also includes celebrating who you are. Once you have moved from knowing yourself and accepting yourself, you can begin to learn how to celebrate yourself. Celebrate the way that God has made you. Celebrate your birthday and your unique personality with its desires. Celebrate your distinctive background and experiences. As you begin to know, accept, and celebrate who you are, you will be more comfortable with knowing, accepting, and celebrating others.

Being loving involves loving yourself. You cannot love others well until you begin to love yourself. By this, I mean loving not from a selfish perspective, but from a healthy perspective. God created you with a specific purpose in mind and He wants you to be appreciative of who He created you to be. He did not make a mistake when He made you. I encourage you to pursue the process of learning to love yourself.

Personal Reflection Questions

1. What are three things that you have grown to know about yourself over the past year?

2. What do you need to accept about yourself that will not change, as it is who God created you to be?

3. What do you love about who God has created you to be? How can you personally begin to celebrate that part of who you are?

Today's Prayer: *God, thank you for making me who I am. I know that you have placed me here on this earth for a reason with a specific design. I thank you for my parents because you used them to bring me into this world. Lord, help me to grow in knowing myself so that I can be who you created me to be. I ask for your grace to be able to accept all of who I am without shame or regret. I ask for the freedom to celebrate who you have made me to be without guilt, or explanation. Lord, help me to be me.*

Statement of Being: Today, I will choose to *"be loving"* to myself because I am lovable.

WEEK 4

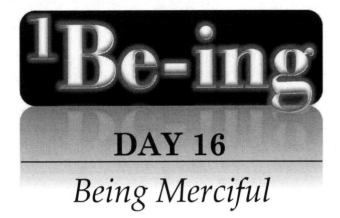

DAY 16

Being Merciful

Main Entry: ¹mer·ci·ful

Pronunciation: \'mər-si-fəl\

Function: *adjective*

Definition: full of compassion or forbearance especially to an offender or to one subject to one's power

³⁶ *Be merciful, just as your Father is merciful. (Luke 6:36)*

B EING MERCIFUL IS THE STATE OF BEING ONE WHO IS FULL OF compassion or forbearance, especially to an offender, or to one subject to the power of another. God is merciful in that He is full of compassion to us as offenders who are subject to His power. Since we are created in his image, being merciful is part of being who God has created us to be. God is looking for people who will demonstrate His mercy to others because He has demonstrated His mercy to them. The mercy that God has demonstrated in our lives provides the perspective we need to extend mercy to others.

12 Speak and act as those who are going to be judged by the law that gives freedom, 13 because judgment without mercy will be shown to anyone who has not been merciful. Mercy triumphs over judgment! (James 2:12-13)

For nearly eighteen years, I struggled with an area of sin management in my life that I could not seem to shake. I prayed, I fasted, I cried and I tried, but after years, this area of sin continued to plague my life. God was using me to minister to others in various formats and venues, and though I could see their liberation, I struggled to grasp my own. After eighteen years, I finally began to gain some level of victory in this area through prayer and accountability. After beginning to walk in some level of victory, I noticed that I was a different person. Prior to going through this struggle, I was a judgmental person who felt that everyone needed to stop sinning and "get their act together." Yes, sin is a choice, but often we struggle to make the right choices consistently. In the moment when we are struggling, we need to have the mercy of God, and His people, extended to us.

I am thankful that I have friends and family members who listen, pray for me, and allow me to experience the true mercy of God in a unique way. Now, as a staff pastor at a local church, I come into contact with people from various backgrounds that have had various experiences. Their life journey has formed and shaped them. When someone comes into my office and shares their struggles, or perceived failures, I could easily choose to be judgmental, especially if they are struggling to honor God in a specific area of their life. Yet, I cannot do so with a clear conscious. I too, have made poor choices when I was in need of God's mercy. Because I have experienced His mercy on a personal level, I am able to extend His mercy.

James teaches us that we should speak and act as if we are going to be judged by the law that gives freedom; not a law that continues to bring bondage. When we judge others without extending God's mercy, we miss the opportunity to receive the mercy that God has made available to us. As a believer in Christ, each of us has been extended significant mercy that we could not repay. We have withdrawn so much mercy from our mercy accounts, that we could easily bounce checks of mercy every day, but His mercy is newly available each day.

As believers in Christ, nothing demonstrates God's love in a more practical way than to extend the mercy of God to people who are further from the Father. Everyone knows when they are doing wrong; they need someone that can love them and extend mercy while they are growing to do what is right. Think about it, would you rather receive judgment or mercy? Mercy is what you need, though judgment is what you deserve. The mercy of God is what makes Christianity so unique and special. We serve a God who extends mercy and grace to us in our time of need.

[14] Therefore, since we have a great high priest who has gone through the heavens, Jesus the Son of God, let us hold firmly to the faith we profess. [15] For we do not have a high priest who is unable to sympathize with our weaknesses, but we have one who has been tempted in every way, just as we are--yet was without sin. [16] Let us then approach the throne of grace with confidence, so that we may receive mercy and find grace to help us in our time of need. (Hebrews 4:14-16)

Personal Reflection Questions

1. Reflect on a time in your life when you received mercy instead of judgment. How did that change your approach to extending mercy to others?

2. Draw a word picture that describes what mercy means to you.

3. Do you approach God with confidence as to find mercy and grace in the time of need? If so, how did you get to the point where you were able to do so? If not, what is hindering you from coming to God with confidence?

Today's Prayer: *God, thank you for the mercy you have extended to me in moments of my life where I willfully chose to dishonor you and your parameters for my life. Thank you for sending Jesus to be the high priest who can sympathize with my struggles and provide the grace and mercy I need. I ask that you will help me come to you with confidence and to extend the mercy that I have received from you unto others.*

Statement of Being: Today, I will choose to be merciful because God has graciously extended His unlimited mercy to me.

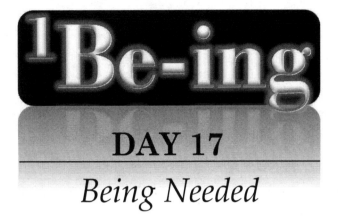

DAY 17

Being Needed

Main Entry: ¹need·ed
Pronunciation: \ 'nēd-əd \
Function: *adjective*
Definition: To be necessary

¹⁴ Now the body is not made up of one part but of many. ¹⁵ If the foot should say, "Because I am not a hand, I do not belong to the body," it would not for that reason cease to be part of the body. ¹⁶ And if the ear should say, "Because I am not an eye, I do not belong to the body," it would not for that reason cease to be part of the body. ¹⁷ If the whole body were an eye, where would the sense of hearing be? If the whole body were an ear, where would the sense of smell be? ¹⁸ But in fact God has arranged the parts in the body, every one of them, just as he wanted them to be. ¹⁹ If they were all one part, where would the body be? ²⁰ As it is, there are many parts, but one body. ²⁷ Now you are the body of Christ, and each one of you is a part of it. (1 Corinthians 12:14-20; 27)

B EING NEEDED IS STATE OF BEING ONE THAT IS NECESSARY. Have you ever viewed yourself as a necessity? I can see the perplexed look on your face. I am not talking about people needing you to do something for them . . . I am sure you have had enough of that in your life. I am talking about the body of Christ needing you to be whole and complete. Paul speaks to the Church at Corinth and He uses the metaphor of a physical body to describe the spiritual body of Christ. Every person that comes to Christ has a role within the body of Christ that is necessary for the body to function properly. When you do not understand or embrace your necessity to the body of Christ through serving in a ministry, the body of Christ is incomplete.

How would you feel if your hand decided it was not going to serve for a year because it had some other things it needed to focus on right now? You would feel surprised, sad, disappointed and upset. I can imagine that your heart would be so hurt. Without a hand that works, you would be identified and labeled as a person with a disability. When we choose not to serve our role in the body of Christ, we cause the body of Christ to be disabled.

The body of Christ needs your ministry and since you are a part of the body, you need your ministry. There is a level of fulfillment and freedom that you will never experience, until you begin to serve God through the venue of a local community of faith. Here you will be connected to the other members of the body and functioning in harmony.

If you are believer in Christ, but have not yet committed to a local church in your area, I challenge you to join that part of the body. An expression of Christ's body in your community needs your part of the body to be healthy. As a believer, you are given spiritual gifts at your spiritual conception. Since you have been given spiritual gifts, your community of faith needs you to use those gifts to help your church express God's love fully in your community.

How would feel if as a parent, you gave your child a brand new car for graduation and a week later when you needed a ride, they said, "I cannot give *you* a ride, this is *my* car?"? Relax - this is a hypothetical situation. But you can sense the level of disappointment and confusion that you would have if you had given your child a gift that you could not benefit from. Similarly, God has given you a gift and He wants you to use it for His glory within a local body of Christ. No matter who you are and what you feel you have to offer, you are needed in the body of Christ because "you *are* the body of Christ. *Everyone* is a part of it."

Personal Reflection Questions:

1. How does it make you feel to know that you are needed by the body of Christ?

2. Reflect on a time in your life where you were able to be a part of something bigger than yourself and where you contributed something that made the entire process effective. What was your role and how did you feel being a part of a bigger picture?

3. If you are not a member of a local church, what is hindering you from committing to membership? How can you invite God to give you what you need to make that commitment?

Today's Prayer: *Lord, I today I want to accept the gift of being one that is needed by the body of Christ. I realize that I have something to offer the body of Christ in order for it to be fully functional. I do not want to cause my local community of faith to be disabled, so I pray that you would open my eyes to see where you are calling me to serve. Give me the courage and confidence to be the part of the body you have created me to be.*

Statement of Being: Today, I will choose to be needed because the body of Christ needs me to be fully functional and effective in being Christ's body on earth.

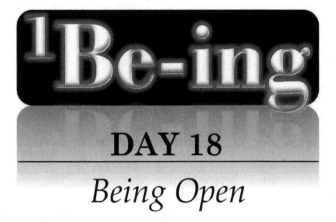

DAY 18

Being Open

Main Entry: ¹open
Pronunciation: \ˈō-pən\
Function: *adjective*
Definition: having no enclosing or confining barrier: accessible on all or nearly all sides

All my longings lie open before you, O Lord; (Psalm 38:9)

BEING OPEN IS THE STATE OF NOT HAVING AN ENCLOSING OR confining barrier; therefore being accessible on all, or nearly all sides. David was one of the most open people mentioned in all of Scripture. Often times, because we have been hurt, or damaged in some way, we begin to close ourselves to the possibilities of God doing something unique or special in our lives. We live daily believing that life is going to continue to be the same status quo situation. But today I want to challenge to be open by removing barriers that keep you from what God may want do in your life.

Being open involves . . .

BEING OPEN TO GOD

Have you ever noticed how easy it is to try to put God in a box? For some reason, we like having a God that we can manage or control. So, we put God in a box based on our past experiences with Him and His people. If we have never seen God provide miraculously, we believe that it only happens to other people. If we have never seen God heal instantaneously, we believe that it only happens on "those-kind-of" television shows. If we have never seen God use our gifts to help someone else, we believe it only happens to the most gifted people. Today I want to challenge you to be open to God doing something that He has never done in your life before. Place your longings before Him and give Him the space to surprise you with His love, mercy and kindness. What do you have to lose? God can do exceedingly, abundantly above all that we can ask or imagine according to the power that is at work in us. Be open and watch God move.

BEING OPEN TO OPPORTUNITIES

We have heard the cliché, "If it seems too good to be true, than it probably is." There is wisdom in this statement. Obviously, there are some opportunities that could hinder us, instead of help us. Despite this fact, I want to challenge you to be open to opportunities that God brings into your life. If you receive an offer for a job that you do not feel qualified for, be open in pursuing it, and see what happens. You never know what could happen. If someone wants to invite you to lunch to have a conversation, be open as to what that conversation may bring into your life. We cannot receive what God has for us with closed hands, hearts, and minds. We must be open to opportunities that arise.

When I was a senior in college, one of my mentors invited me to consider serving in full-time, college ministry right after graduation. I was closed - not open to the opportunity because it involved raising financial support and I did not believe that people would give to support my ministry. I was thinking, "I did not go to college for five years to ask people for money to pay my salary." I passed up the opportunity for a year and found myself working at a job that I did not enjoy as much. I was working during the day and volunteering to teach bible study on campus multiple times a week outside of my job. In the end, the opportunity remained available and a year later, I accepted it. College ministry became the foundation of my ministry training and experience. Even if I would have ultimately said no, I should have been more open to what the opportunity presented.

BEING OPEN TO LOVE

We were created to love and be loved, but in society we experience a great deal of hurt. Because of this, we put up the biggest barriers in regards to loving others and *being loved by* others. If you are a man that has no friends, you need to consider being open to fellowship with other men who can encourage and empower you as you become the man that God wants you to be. If you are a woman who has written off friendships with other women because of negative experiences in the past, I challenge you to be open to God bringing a godly friend into your life who can be a true confidant and companion in your journey. You never know how God could use the power of friendship to form a more desirable future.

If you are a single person that wants to be in a relationship, be open to the people that God is bringing into your life. Begin by engaging in a godly, open friendship. You never know who God may want to bring into your life in this season or in seasons to come. Without being open, you will push every possibility away, only protecting yourself from pain and all the while keeping yourself from the possibility of a purposeful relationship. Even if the relationship does not work out, you have not failed; you have simply eliminated one other person from the possibilities of long-term relationships.

I remember when I first met my wife. I was leading the gospel choir and greeting all the new members at an ice skating rink. A year later, she was beginning to serve in leadership with the choir and we started to get to know one another. We were both willing to be open. After a number of weeks getting to know each other and being in one another's company, we prayerfully entered into a dating relationship that ultimately led to the most fulfilling relationship we have had outside of our relationship with Christ. Marriage! Will it happen like that for you? I do not know, but I do know it will *not* happen if you are not being open to love.

Personal Reflection Questions:

1. In what area of your relationship with God do you need to be more open?

2. What opportunities are currently being offered to you that you need to consider being open to receive?

3. Where is God sending love your way that you need to be open to receiving in this season of your life?

Today's Prayer: *Lord, I want to be open, but at times I am scared. The pain of the past will keep me from the present if I allow it to. I am asking you to give me the wisdom and discernment to know when and how to be more open to you, to opportunities, and to love in my life. I know that I cannot receive what you have for me by being closed to the possibility of what you want to do in my life. I ask that you will help me trust in you completely so that I will become open.*

Statement of Being: Today, I will choose to be open because I cannot walk through a closed door.

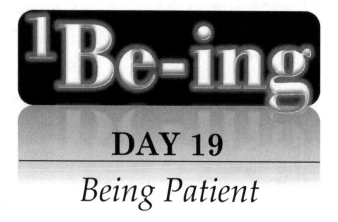

DAY 19

Being Patient

Main Entry: ¹pa·tient
Pronunciation: \'pā-shənt\
Function: *adjective*
Definition: bearing pains or trials calmly or without complaint

²² *But the fruit of the Spirit is . . . patience. (Galatians 5:22)*

BEING PATIENT IS THE STATE BEING ONE THAT BEARS PAINS or trials calmly, or without complaint. Patience is one of the most limited resources in our current society. We live in a culture that teaches us that we can have it our way, right away. The microwave mentality of our culture teaches us we can have the benefits of something that normally requires a long-term, but in a limited amount of time. We want a deep, romantic relationship to develop in a matter of two weeks and we want our stocks to appreciate in one year. We want a get-rich-quick-scheme to solve all of our financial problems and we want to be healed from being hurt overnight. The challenge with this mindset is that it creates an unrealistic expectation that can rarely be met. If you become an overnight success, it is likely that you will not have the character to maintain the level of success you gain while you were sleeping.

God is a patient God and since we are created in his image, being patient is a part of what it means to be who God created us to be. My pastor often says, "God is never in a hurry." God does not rush because he lives outside of time in eternity, only looking into time to manifest what has already happened in eternity. *In Isaiah 46:10 God says, "I make known the end from the beginning, from ancient times, what is still to come. I say: My purpose will stand, and I will do all that I please."* God has already seen what is going to happen on this side. With that in mind, I want to challenge you consider how to be patient.

Being patient involves . . .

Actively Waiting

"[7]Be patient, then, brothers, until the Lord's coming. See how the farmer waits for the land to yield its valuable crop and how patient he is for the autumn and spring rains. [8] You too, be patient and stand firm, because the Lord's coming is near." (James 5:7-8)

For some reason, we often embrace one extreme or the other when it comes to patience. We either wait for something to happen while doing nothing, or we rush into doing something without waiting. The farmer plants his seed and waters it while he waits for it to grow. When the seeds are harvested, he allows the land to rest so it can be ready for the following season. While it is resting, he adds nutrients and fertilizers that will assist the land in being ready for the following season. Being patient involves actively waiting. If you are being patient about getting married, you want to wait actively through developing your personal spiritual life, pursuing your God-given purpose, and developing your relational skills. If you are being patient when it comes to starting your own business, you want to wait actively through being faithful to your current job, building relationships with others who are interested in your business, and learning how to manage the influence that you will ultimately have in the new role. Active waiting prepares you to receive what God has for you when He brings it to you.

Quietly Enduring

6 If we are distressed, it is for your comfort and salvation; if we are comforted, it is for your comfort, which produces in you patient endurance of the same sufferings we suffer. 7 And our hope for you is firm, because we know that just as you share in our sufferings, so also you share in our comfort. (2 Corinthians 1:6-7)

Patience is characterized by bearing pains without complaining. I encourage you to engage in an exercise the next time you have to extend yourself beyond your normal limits. Try going through an entire day without complaining. Often our complaint is a way of us asking for sympathy or appreciation for our sacrifice or pain. We want others to feel for us, instead of choosing to be a model of patience; enduring without complaining.

When I was in the 9th grade, my mother was diagnosed with renal failure, meaning that her kidneys would not flush toxins out of her body. Due to other health complications, she was not in the best shape to handle a transplant. She was given two other options: 1) three-and-half hour, three times a week treatment on a dialysis machine for the rest of her life, or 2) dying within a short amount of time and missing what life had to offer in the future. Her diagnosis was over 15 years ago. She has quietly endured the weekly regiment of having a needle stuck in her arm and having to sit in a chair for three-and-half hours while a machine does what her kidneys were created to do. When I see her go through this day in and day out, I am reminded of Jesus who endured the cross without saying a word in His defense. He quietly endured the cross so we could quietly endure our struggles through His power.

Humbly Receiving
[2] *Be completely humble and gentle; be patient, bearing with one another in love. (Ephesians 4:2)*

When you have actively waited and quietly endured, you are able to receive what you have waited for with humility. You realize that being patient is part of the gift that God is trying to give you all along. God's delay does not always mean denial; often it means development. During the active waiting season, God develops the character needed to handle the blessing He will bring. During the quiet, enduring season, God develops the perseverance needed to handle the next challenge that comes your way. Then, you will be able to receive the gift of God with humility, knowing that it was God who gave it to you, and it is God who will empower you through His Spirit to maintain the blessing. The process of actively waiting and quietly enduring, also equips you to be patient with others as you see them grow in their development. You know what it was like to move through the stages of preparation and perseverance to get where you are. You can grow from being a champion for your own development, to being a coach for someone else. What a testimony not only to receive a gift from God, but through patience, be able to give that gift to someone else.

Personal Reflection Questions

1. What is the activity God is calling you to do as you wait for what He has promised you?

2. What have you had to endure to be where you are today? Were you able to quietly endure? What would you do differently if you had to endure the situation again?

3. If you were to actively wait and quietly endure, what do you believe you could humbly receive?

Today's Prayer: *Father, I know that you have prepared what is best for me. Your timing is perfect and you are working out the details of my life according to your ultimate plan. In the process of being patient, help me to actively wait, quietly endure, and humbly receive what you have for me, trusting that you will bring all that I need in your time.*

Statement of Being: Today, I will choose to be patient because the right thing at the wrong time is the wrong thing.

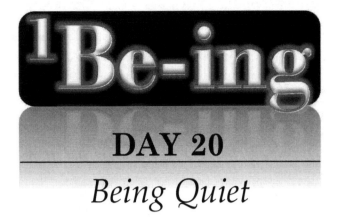

DAY 20

Being Quiet

Main Entry: ¹quiet
Pronunciation: \ˈkwī-ət\
Function: *adjective*
Definition: marked by little or no motion or activity

[15] *This is what the Sovereign LORD, the Holy One of Israel, says: "In repentance and rest is your salvation, in quietness and trust is your strength, but you would have none of it." (Isaiah 30:15)*

BEING QUIET IS STATE OF BEING ONE WHO IS MARKED BY little, or no motion, or activity. Ironically, we continue to focus on being quiet after sharing the importance of active waiting. There is a balance between being quiet and being patient, as it yields great fruit in the life of the Spirit. God has a way of speaking when we are quiet. It is interesting in the English language that the word "silent" and the word "listen" use the same letters to create different words. God has a sense of humor. When we are silent, we can actually listen.

Isaiah reminds us that our strength comes in quietness and trust. Being quiet is one of the ways that we demonstrate our trust in God. We do not feel the need to always have something to say, but we can sit in a room and be silent, allowing God to speak to us either through His word or through our spirit. I have learned that if I am willing to be quiet long enough, I will hear words from God that I thought I needed to hear from other people. When I am quiet, I hear God say, "I love you, my son." When I am quiet, I hear God say, "I am proud of who you are becoming." When I am quiet, I hear God say, "Well done!" Often the approval and affirmation we think we need from the crowd can be heard most clearly from the creator in a moment of quietness.

Being Quiet involves having . . .

A QUIET MOUTH
"19 My dear brothers, take note of this: Everyone should be quick to listen, slow to speak . . ." (James 1:19)

A quiet mouth begins the process of being silent. When we learn to limit our verbal expressions through words, we can learn to hear what someone else has to say. I have often heard it said - if you are the smartest person in the room, you need to find another room. If this statement is true, then we do not know whether we are the smartest person in the room until we quiet our mouths to hear what someone else has to say. We already know what we know; we need to know what they know. So, I encourage you to consider taking five minutes today to engage in quieting your mouth to see what you hear.

A QUIET MIND

² *How long must I wrestle with my thoughts and every day have sorrow in my heart? (Psalm 13:2)*

In a society that offers so much noise, having a quiet mind is even more challenging than having a quiet mouth. We can close our mouths and not say a word, but still have the noise reverberating in our minds. The noise of a song we heard on radio or the noise of a compliment we heard on the job. We hear the noise of our meetings from the day as we replay them over in our minds, thinking about what we could have done differently. Before you know it, the mind can be louder than the mouth. David identifies with us by asking the question, how long must I wrestle with my thoughts? The spiritual disciplines of silence and solitude allow us to practice and develop a quiet mind through the Spirit's power. It quiets our minds so we can have peace of mind and clarity of thought.

A QUIET SPIRIT

³ *Your beauty should not come from outward adornment, such as braided hair and the wearing of gold jewelry and fine clothes.* ⁴ *Instead, it should be that of your inner self, the unfading beauty of a gentle and quiet spirit, which is of great worth in God's sight. (1 Peter 3:15)*

A quiet spirit is the result of a quiet mouth and a quiet mind. Peter teaches women in the New Testament church that their beauty is not found in their outward appearance, but rather in their gentle and quiet spirit which is of great worth in God's sight. There are few people that I know with quiet spirits, but most of them are people who have been living for a while. Their lives have taught them the value of being still and knowing God. There is a depth to the well of their soul that was not dug in a day, but over a lifetime. You can hear the stillness of their spirit anytime you are in their presence and somehow they have a way of bringing calmness to all who are around them. Their perspective on life is broad enough to include God's intervention and simple enough to accept His delays. Their lives are steady and stable. In many ways, the seasoned saints in my life have become my role models because I know that to lead a life that is lived well, I must consistently seek to have a spirit that is quiet and still in the midst of a storm.

Personal Reflection Questions

1. If you struggle to be quiet, to what do you attribute the struggle? How can you begin to take steps to quiet your mouth, mind and spirit?

2. What is one thing you can do consistently to quiet your mind?

3. Who is someone in your life that has modeled a quiet spirit? I encourage you to make plans this weekend to call them, or take them out to dinner and invite them to share their wisdom in developing a quiet spirit.

Today's Prayer: *God, if my strength comes from being quiet, then being quiet is a must in every season of my life. Teach me to daily quiet my mouth, mind and spirit, as I know that when I am quiet, I will be able hear more clearly, your still, small voice that speaks and provides direction for my life. Thank you for being a speaking God that speaks today.*

Statement of Being: Today, I will choose to be quiet so I can more clearly hear God's voice.

WEEK 5

DAY 21

Being Reconciled
Part 1

Main Entry: ¹rec·on·ciled
Pronunciation: \ ˈre-kən-ˌsī(-ə)ld \
Function: *adjective*
Definition: being restored to friendship or harmony

¹⁶ So from now on we regard no one from a worldly point of view. Though we once regarded Christ in this way, we do so no longer. ¹⁷ Therefore, if anyone is in Christ, he is a new creation; the old has gone, the new has come! ¹⁸ All this is from God, who reconciled us to himself through Christ and gave us the ministry of reconciliation: ¹⁹ that God was reconciling the world to himself in Christ, not counting men's sins against them. And he has committed to us the message of reconciliation. ²⁰ We are therefore Christ's ambassadors, as though God were making his appeal through us. We implore you on Christ's behalf: Be reconciled to God. ²¹ God made him who had no sin to be sin for us, so that in him we might become the righteousness of God. (2 Corinthians 5:16-21)

BEING RECONCILED IS THE STATE OF BEING ONE WHO HAS been restored to a friendship, or has harmony in a relationship. When we were born into this world, we were distanced from God due to the separating factor of sin. God is holy and cannot be in relationship with someone who is not holy. He sent His holy son Jesus to die on the cross for our sins so that we could be reconciled to him through the sacrifice of His Son. If you have chosen to do that, you are now reconciled. You have been restored to a right relationship and friendship with God in a place where there is harmony and peace. So, now that you are reconciled, how are you to live?

Being reconciled involves:

LIVING A NEW LIFE

Often at our church, I have privilege of leading someone into the life-changing experience of becoming a new believer in Christ. As any believer can tell you, after a day or two often there seems to be some sort of negative thought pattern that causes you to question whether you are really saved. The enemy wants the new believer to question their salvation. Satan often uses the strategy of telling new believers that they are not saved because God could never forgive them of what they have done in the past. Paul reminds us in our passage for today, that once we are in Christ, we are a new creation, the old has gone and the new has come. We have been born again into a new life and our lives will not be the same as the old life we lived. We may have to grow in freedom from some areas of sin that previously held us captive, but in the mind of God we are already a new creation with a new life.

The reality of being a new creation reminds me of one of my favorite TV shows that features a witness protection program. When someone has witnessed a crime and their lives are in danger due to their knowledge of the crime, the government would relocate them to another area in the country, giving them a new name, a new role and a new start on life. They are able to begin again with a clean slate that is blank for them to write a new chapter in their lives. Similarly when we come to Christ, the enemy is looking to take us out because we have testified on the witness stand of our hearts that Jesus is Lord. Jesus puts our old life in the past and gives us a new name, a new role and a new start on life. If you are a person constantly reminded of your past, I want to encourage you to live a new life because you have been reconciled with God.

SHARING A NEW MESSAGE

Now that you have been reconciled to God, He wants to give you a new message to share with everyone in your world. Often new Christians become isolated from their old friends in order to establish their new life in Christ and I understand the rationale behind this choice; but I believe that God saved you so that you could go back to your old friends and share a new message that Paul describes as the message of reconciliation. The message is that Christ, who knew no sin, became sin for us so that we might become the righteousness of God through Him. To put it simply, Christ died in our place. He took the death penalty so we could have new life. Who better to demonstrate the life-changing power of Christ to your old friends than you as a new creation in Christ? Nothing speaks louder than a changed life. You could be the before and after picture that someone needs to see to consider trusting Christ. The New Testament writer Paul is a perfect example of someone who became a new creation in Christ and lived the second half

121

of his life more meaningfully than the first half. I encourage you the share the new message that you have received with everyone that God has placed in your life.

RECEIVING A NEW ASSIGNMENT

Now that you are a new creation and you have received a new message, you are on a new assignment. I do not know what your life was like before Christ, but I can tell you that this new assignment is the most prestigious role you could ever wish for. Christ has given you the distinct honor of being one of His ambassadors. An ambassador is one who represents his nation in a foreign country. He often works in an embassy that is considered part of his home country. He works with those in the foreign land to advance the interests of his country in their land. That is what Christ has called you to do. He has called you to live in a world that is a foreign land because Heaven is your new home. You are called to live in the embassy of your body while you are in this foreign land on earth. Now you have the privilege of using all of the resources in gifts and abilities that God has given you to advance His kingdom on earth. What a signature honor to be an ambassador of the King of Kings and the Lord of Lords. His kingdom will never fail and He will reign forever. So get used to your new assignment and do all you can to advance the kingdom of God on earth.

Personal Reflection Questions

1. Reflect on your new life in Christ. How did you change the most when you came to know Christ?

122

2. How comfortable are you with sharing the new message you have received . . . the message of reconciliation? What would make you more comfortable with sharing the new message of reconciliation?

3. As Christ's ambassador, how are you choosing to live differently than before coming to Christ?

Today's Prayer: *Lord, I am so glad that you made me a new creation when I chose to accept you as my Savior. I remember what my life was like before you intersected my journey and I want to take this moment to say thank you for saving me. I pray that I will be the type of ambassador that brings you joy through the way I represent you in this foreign land. Give me the courage to share the message of reconciliation because I know the benefits of knowing you.*

Statement of Being: Today, I will choose to live as a new creation because my old life is history.

DAY 22

Being Reconciled Part 2

²⁰ *"My prayer is not for them alone. I pray also for those who will believe in me through their message,* ²¹ *that all of them may be one, Father, just as you are in me and I am in you. May they also be in us so that the world may believe that you have sent me.* ²² *I have given them the glory that you gave me, that they may be one as we are one:* ²³ *I in them and you in me. May they be brought to complete unity to let the world know that you sent me and have loved them even as you have loved me. (John 17:20-23)*

TODAY, AS WE CONTINUE CONSIDERING THE STATE OF BEING reconciled, I want to invite you to consider the broader implications of the ministry and message of reconciliation. Prior to going to the cross, Jesus prayed for His disciples and those that would believe His message. He prayed that we would be one unified people of faith demonstrating that God sent Jesus to the earth. Our ability to unify says more to people who are far from God than most of our marketing and evangelism strategies. People do not want to *hear* what we believe; they want to *see* what we believe.

As an African-American man who was raised in this country, I have been blessed to have the wonderful opportunity of being connected to people from various racial and ethnic backgrounds. I grew up with two best friends, one was Latin and the other was of European-decent. I spent most of my time with them during the week, but for some reason on Sunday, we worshipped in different places. I later came to realize that the 400-year sin of racism in our nation affected my personal worship experience more than I understood at the time. As I continued to grow and attend college, I began to own more of my ethnic identity and gained a passion for seeing people from different backgrounds reconciled to one another as a result of having been reconciled to Christ.

In our nation, I believe that God is calling believers to consider the implications of reconciliation with Him so that we might make better, informed choices when it comes to personal relationships, corporate worship, and systemic structures in our nation. Jesus died to bridge the greatest chasm in the universe, the chasm formed by sin between humans and God. I believe that Jesus also died to bridge the greatest chasm in our nation, the chasm of racial division. I want to share a few ways we can consider being reconciled to one another to demonstrate God's love and power of reconciliation to people who have yet to know Christ.

Being Racially-Reconciled involves . . .

SEEKING GOD

I learned a long time ago that racial reconciliation is not something that we establish by using only our human nature.

This giant is one that must be slain in the Spirit. We must spend time in prayer asking God to reveal our hearts and our hurts so that we can allow Him to use us in the process of bringing about healing. I know that many of us have had negative experiences with people from different backgrounds that have made us afraid and angry. Others have had limited experiences with people from different backgrounds which have made them ignorant or insensitive. Still, others have had some experiences with people from different backgrounds that have made them unaware and apathetic. As believers in Christ, we must do business with God and ask what He wants us to do to be the answer to Christ's prayer of unity amongst His body. As we pray I believe God will reveal the depths of our hearts and give us a vision for what He sees in this area of reconciliation.

SHARING EXPERIENCES

As we are praying, we can actively pursue personal relationships with individuals and groups that allow us to learn about our brothers and sisters in Christ. We need to begin by sharing similar experiences. If you are a mother, you can relate to other mothers. If you are a sports fan, you can relate to another sports fan. The beauty of this calling is that reconciliation is not the same as assimilation. God is calling us to be who we are while being in harmony with people who are different from us. Contrary to some popular belief, we have many differences between us. Each of our upbringings is uniquely based in our ethnic, socio-economic, geographic, educational, and spiritual backgrounds. There are many lenses responsible for framing our view of the world, but despite each of those lenses, we see some things the same. So, begin by sharing similar experiences with someone in your neighborhood, on your job, or in your church as a bridge builder to a personal relationship.

SACRIFICING SOMETHING

In Acts 2, we see a community of faith that is more unified than any community of faith that we have seen since the 1ˢᵗ century church. The members shared everything in common by giving resources to make sure everyone had what they needed. Sacrificing is counter-cultural to our *American* way of life, but it should be a normal part of our *Christian* way of life. In order for true reconciliation to prevail, we all have to sacrifice something. We might have to sacrifice power or position. We might have to sacrifice privileges or personal preferences. The biblical model of reconciliation demonstrates that there can be no atonement without a sacrifice. Jesus had to sacrifice His home in Heaven to come to earth so we could eventually leave our lives here on earth and join him in Heaven. Jesus also had to sacrifice the power to free Himself from the cross to give us power over sin and death. We will all need to sacrifice to see racial reconciliation become a reality in our lifetime; but like the 1ˢᵗ Century church in Acts, I know the sacrifice will be worth it.

SALVATION

Because Christ was willing to sacrifice, many were saved including the man who died next to Him on the cross. I believe when we choose to seek God, share experiences, and sacrifice, we will see people from every nation and tongue coming, not only to Christ, but coming together to demonstrate Christ's saving power. They will see not only the salvation of an individual soul, but of an entire group of people who have called on His name.

⁹ After this I looked and there before me was a great multitude that no one could count, from every nation, tribe, people and language, standing before the throne and in front of the Lamb. They were wearing white robes and were holding palm branches in their hands. ¹⁰ And they cried out in a loud voice: "Salvation belongs to our God, who sits on the throne, and to the Lamb." (Revelation 7:9-10)

For some reason, John left us a glimpse of a unified worship experience in heaven with people from every nation, tribe and language standing before the throne of God crying out about His salvation. I believe that God is calling us as nation to provide a preview of this main attraction by choosing to reconcile with one another because we are reconciled to God through Christ.

Personal Reflection Questions

1. Reflect on the experiences you have had with people from various racial and ethnic backgrounds. What gifts have you gained from someone that was different from you ethnically?

2. Think of the friends you have from different racial or ethnic backgrounds. What do you have in common that allows you to connect with one another? How can this be a building block for a deeper friendship?

3. What is God calling you to sacrifice in order to be reconciled with someone from a different racial or ethnic background?

Today's Prayer: *God, I acknowledge that racial differences have divided Christians in our nation and I admit that I have, in some way, contributed to this divide. I ask that you will search my heart and give me insight into what you are calling me to do in response to your message of reconciliation, extending from salvation to a united kingdom of God here on earth. Help me to be honest with myself and honest with others in doing my part to be reconciled.*

Statement of Being: Today, I will choose to be reconciled through opening my eyes to see all of God's people as my brothers and sisters in Christ.

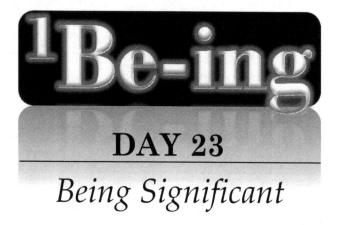

DAY 23

Being Significant

Main Entry: ¹sig·nif·i·cant
Pronunciation: \-kənt\
Function: *adjective*
Definition: having meaning

¹⁰ The thief comes only to steal and kill and destroy; I have come that they may have life, and have it to the full. (John 10:10)

BEING SIGNIFICANT IS THE STATE OF BEING ONE WHO HAS meaning in their life. Significance comes from understanding your place in life. We often struggle between the question of pursuing significance, or success, but I believe that when you find significance, you find success. Jesus teaches that He came to give you life to the full. Full life is a life that is full of meaning because of who you are and whose you are. You find significance when you discover who God has created you to be and then in response, you begin doing what God created you to do.

For we are God's workmanship, created in Christ Jesus to do good works, which God prepared in advance for us to do. (Ephesians 2:10)

Once you discover that you were created in Christ to do something that has already been prepared by God, you can find the meaning of your life. I know there is a reason for your life, because you are here. God brings each person into the world to fulfill a purpose that only they can fulfill. The question to ask is, "Why am I here? Who has God created me to be and what does God want me to do?"

There is both a general and specific answer to this question. I cannot answer the specific question for you; that is something that God has to do, but I can answer the general question of why you are here. You are here to love God and love other people. It is that simple. If you are looking for meaning in life, I encourage you to do all you can to love God. Spend time in prayer, reading Scripture, and worshipping him. Spend time seeking His nature and His heart. Find out what He desires and what makes Him smile.

Out of the moments you spend with God and based on the way that He has formed you, I encourage you to love others. Begin giving back in a way that allows you to use your gifts. Begin sharing your life with other people through meaningful conversations and experiences. Begin asking questions of others and seeking answers. As you learn to love God and love other people, you will discover significance in the natural flow of life. I encourage you to try it for the next seven days. Each night after you have passionately loved God and those around you, ask yourself one question, "How did I add value to someone else's life today?" When you begin to see the answer to that question, you will begin to find the significance that you bring to life.

Personal Reflection Questions

1. Would you describe your life as empty, half-full or full? What is the missing piece you need to find significance?

2. How will you choose to personally add value to someone you know today?

3. Who have you been longing to have a meaningful conversation with? Choose to give them a call this week and invite them to share with you. Listen and watch God work.

Today's Prayer: *Lord, I acknowledge that my significance comes from you. It is so easy to put value on what others think or need from me, instead of what you think of me. Today I pray for a renewed sense of significance. Help me to find meaning in life and add meaning to the lives of others. I ask for the grace to be significant today.*

Statement of Being: Today, I will choose to be significant because God has given me meaning in life.

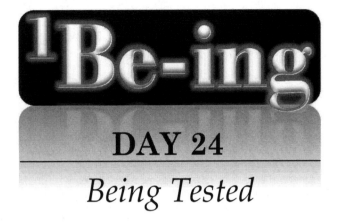

DAY 24

Being Tested

Main Entry: test·ed
Pronunciation: \ 'tes-təd \
Function: *adjective*
Definition: subjected to or qualified through testing

[2] Consider it pure joy, my brothers, whenever you face trials of many kinds, [3] because you know that the testing of your faith develops perseverance. [4] Perseverance must finish its work so that you may be mature and complete, not lacking anything. (James 1:2-4)

BEING TESTED IS THE STATE OF BEING ONE THAT IS SUBJECT TO or qualified through testing. Do you remember taking tests in school? A test was designed to help you discover how much you actually knew about the subject matter. No matter how much you listened in class, read your books and did your homework, the true measure of your knowledge was demonstrated through the test. The same is true in our spiritual life. We do not know how much faith we have until we are tested.

God has given each of us a measure of faith that we are encouraged to develop. You might have more faith than someone else, but you will be tested based on the measure of faith you have. When you are tested, you are given the opportunity to discover if your faith level matches your test level. If you so, you pass go, collect $200 and prepare for the next test. If your faith level does not match the level of your test, you do not pass go or collect $200, and you get to experience that test again. The test may come in a different person, problem or pressure, but the test will resurface again. God is a wonderful teacher. He will not do you the injustice of passing you to the next grade level without knowing that you can handle the new devil.

James teaches us to consider it the purest form of joy when we are tested, as our faith develops perseverance. Perseverance is the ability to remain under pressure without breaking. God wants to develop your strength so that you can handle the pressures of life without breaking. When perseverance is finished, you will be mature and complete not lacking anything. Being mature and complete does not mean you will not make mistakes, because everyone makes mistakes: it is guaranteed in our human contract. Being mature and complete means you do not make the same mistakes over and over again because you learn from the previous tests.

When I was in college, I actually enjoyed tests more than most. I learned to have a positive attitude that began with a positive look. I would wear a suit on test days because I viewed my tests as an interview. The instructor was my potential boss, the subject matter was the company, and I hoped that in my interview – the test – I would prove myself worthy of the job. The suit gave me confidence and the test gave me feedback. I remember earning a grade of 34 on an economics test and realizing that my thorough study methods were not effective. I later made adjustments and passed the class. I was only able to pass because I made midcourse adjustments. In the end, I learned from my mistakes, grew to be more mature and complete in that area by passing economics.

As you consider how you are being tested, remember that God is more committed to your growth than He is to your comfort. He will allow you to be tested until you pass the test, but when you pass the test, you will be stronger than you were before. I encourage you to see your test as an opportunity to interview with God and I pray that you get the job.

Personal Reflection Questions

1. How are you currently being tested?

2. What do you feel God wants you to learn during this test?

3. How are you responding to this lesson?

Today's Prayer: *God, I admit that I really do not like going through tests in life. It would seem easier to learn the lesson without a test, but since that is not usually the case, I pray that you will give me the ability to learn as I go through my test so I can grow through my test. Teach me to seek you during the test and to mature so that I do not continue to make the same mistakes repeatedly. I trust you and I know that you will take care of me so I put my life in your hands during this season of testing. I trust that you will deliver me through.*

Statement of Being: Today, I will choose to be tested because testing provides a platform for my faith to grow.

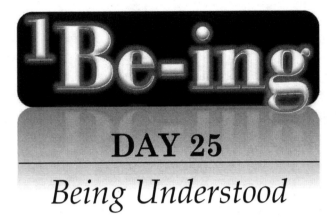

DAY 25

Being Understood

Main Entry: ¹un·der·stood
Pronunciation: \ ˌən-dər-ˈstud \
Function: *adjective*
Definition: fully apprehended

⁴ The word of the LORD came to me, saying, ⁵ "Before I formed you in the womb I knew you, before you were born I set you apart; I appointed you as a prophet to the nations." (Jeremiah 1:4-5)

HAVE YOU EVER BEEN IN A FRIENDSHIP OR A RELATIONSHIP where someone really understood you? A friend that you did not have to explain a whole lot to them, they just got you? They knew your likes and dislikes. They knew your passions and pains. They knew your hopes and dreams. It was as if you knew that no matter how often you were misunderstood, at least this one person understood you. In a world where it is easy to be misunderstood, it is comforting to know that God understands you.

Jeremiah records his experience with coming to know God personally. Jeremiah shares how God informed him that He knew of his existence before he was formed in his mother's womb. God set Jeremiah apart before he was born and appointed him as a prophet to the nations. When we come into a relationship with God, we gain access to the Father who knows us best. God knew you before your conception. In this passage, the word *knew* means to know someone through a shared experience. This knowledge is personal and intimate. God is saying that before your mother and father even knew one another, He knew you intimately. He knew your family and your story line. He knew your personality and your passions. God knew everything about you before you were even conceived.

Then He set you apart. God set you aside for His purpose to accomplish something that only you can accomplish. He appointed you for a significant purpose in this generation. Think about the fact that God knew you would be born in a time of technology and would have the ability to connect with people from around the world instantaneously via the World Wide Web. He dropped you into the world during a season when worldwide travel would be easy by airplanes, cars, and ships. God knew that you would need to live after women's liberation, the civil rights movement, and during the time of American prominence.

Since He understands everything about you and everything about the world you live in, He can identify with you and comfort you. I know that there are times when you feel misunderstood by people that are closest to you. In that moment, I encourage you to be understood by the God of all creation. Allow Him to speak words of comfort in your spirit and words of encouragement in your soul. Allow God to fill that void of being misunderstood with His unlimited knowledge of who you are. In a world where we are often misunderstood, it is comforting to know that God understands us.

Personal Application Questions

1. What does being understood mean to you? How would you describe being understood to a friend or family member?

2. How does it make you feel to know that when no one else understands you, God understands you?

3. In being understood by God, how can you better seek to understand others?

Today's Prayer: *God, what a gift it is to know that I am understood by you. It seems like every day there is a possibility that what I say, or how I look will be misunderstood. In those moments, I will seek comfort in knowing that though I must work to be understood with others, when I am in your presence the effort to be understood can cease. Thank you for knowing me personally and choosing to love me by understanding who I am.*

Statement of Being: Today, I will choose to be understood because God knows me intimately.

WEEK 6

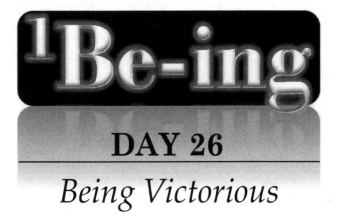

DAY 26

Being Victorious

Main Entry: ¹vic·to·ri·ous
Pronunciation: \ vik-ˈtōr-ē-əs \
Function: *adjective*
Definition: having won a victory by overcoming an enemy or achieving mastery or success in a struggle or endeavor against the odds or difficulties.

⁴ for everyone born of God overcomes the world. This is the victory that has overcome the world, even our faith. ⁵ Who is it that overcomes the world? Only he who believes that Jesus is the Son of God.
(1 John 5:4-5)

B EING VICTORIOUS IS THE STATE OF BEING ONE WHO HAS won a victory by overcoming an enemy, achieving mastery or success in a struggle, or overcoming an endeavor against the odds or difficulties. There are few things that bring more excitement in our country than watching our team win. Every weekend during the fall, millions of people pack stadiums all over this country to watch high school, college and professional football. They spend their hard-earned money

143

to watch their team gain a victory over a rival, or a team that simply wants to beat their team. Fans participate through screaming and yelling to distract the other team. They engage in chants and the waving of towels. They are unified through wearing the same colors and standing for much of the game. All of this effort is designed to help their team gain a victory.

I want you to know that just as there are people rooting for their teams around this nation, God is rooting for you to overcome the struggles in your life. God wants you to be victorious and He is doing all He can to make sure that your victory is won, but you must make some choices to experience victory in your life.

Being victorious involves . . .

FOLLOWING THE GAME PLAN

As we look at John's writing in his first letter, we see that God had a game plan for our victory. His game plan was to send His son Jesus to die for our sins. When we believe that Jesus is the Son of God, we have overcome the world and we become victorious. I noticed that John did not say we would not have to battle on the field or struggle to win, but once we come to know Christ, he said that we will have victory over the world. Believing Jesus is the Son of God means more than believing that He *is* the Son of God. It also means believing in the implications of Him being the Son of God, which means that we will choose to follow His leadership and His game plan for our life. Because of the death and resurrection of Christ, we have gained victory over sin and death. Though we still struggle with sin at times, sin is now a choice, as Christ has removed its controlling power from our lives. Maybe you have struggled with a life controlling issue or have a challenge walking away

144

from a sinful pattern. If this is your experience, I encourage you to claim the victory that Christ made available to you on the cross. Invite Him to fill you with His Spirit and to give you the power to overcome the struggle of sin. Living in a sin pattern compromises our ability to gain long-term victory, but when we obey we feel empowered to overcome and be victorious.

PLAYING WITH A TEAM

The victory that we seek cannot come through playing the game alone. We need to invite others from God's team to assist us in overcoming our struggles. One of the great discoveries of recovery programs is the power of teamwork and accountability. Programs like Alcoholics Anonymous, Narcotics Anonymous and Celebrate Recovery focus on making sure that people who are seeking to gain victory over life controlling issues can have assistance and accountability through a group and a sponsor. The volunteers are people who have gained victory in their own life, so they are able to assist those who struggling while understanding the battle that the person is going through. We all need people in our lives that understand our struggle and encourage us to continue fighting to gain the victory.

DEPENDING ON THE COACH

[3] *It was not by their sword that they won the land,*
    nor did their arm bring them victory;
it was your right hand, your arm,
    and the light of your face, for you loved them.
[4] *You are my King and my God,*
    who decrees victories for Jacob.
[5] *Through you we push back our enemies;*
    through your name we trample our foes.
[6] *I do not trust in my bow,*

> *my sword does not bring me victory;*
> ⁷ *but you give us victory over our enemies,*
> *you put our adversaries to shame.*
> ⁸ *In God we make our boast all day long,*
> *and we will praise your name forever. Selah (Psalm 44:3-8)*

The psalmist in Psalm 44 reminds us where our victory comes from. He says that our victory does not come from our fancy equipment, but from depending on the coach to guide us to victory. No matter how fast we are, or how smart we are, we cannot gain the victory over any area of struggle without the help of God. No matter how much education we have or how many people we know, only God can bring true victory into our lives. Being victorious is closely connected to being dependent, as after gaining a victory in our lives, we need to remain dependent on God to maintain the level of victory we have gained. As soon as we think we have arrived and we no longer need to depend on God to maintain victory, we will find ourselves slipping back into a state of defeat. I pray that you will walk in victory today knowing that Christ has given us victory through our faith in Him. I pray that you will continue to depend on God for the victory that He has brought about in your life and trust Him for future victories that are still to come.

Personal Reflection Questions

1. What area of struggle do you need to claim Christ's victory in your life?

2. Who have you invited to partner with you in the struggle?

3. How can you actively demonstrate your dependence on God for the victory you need?

Today's Prayer: *God, I thank you even though I am fighting in the battle you have already won the war. Through Christ you have given me the victory over sin and death. I pray that I will be victorious today as one who has been set free. I ask that you would give me the humility to partner with other teammates in the struggles I have in life so I can have assistance in gaining victory. I trust you to manifest the victory that has already been won through Christ in my daily life.*

Statement of Being: Today, I will choose to be victorious because the battle is not mine, it is the Lord's.

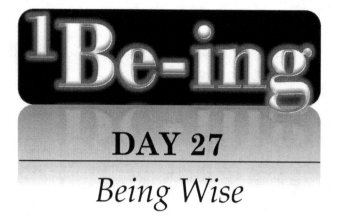

DAY 27

Being Wise

Main Entry: ¹wise
Pronunciation: \ˈwīz\
Function: *adjective*
Definition: characterized by wisdom: marked by deep understanding, keen discernment, and a capacity for sound judgment

If any of you lacks wisdom, he should ask God, who gives generously to all without finding fault, and it will be given to him. ⁶ But when he asks, he must believe and not doubt, because he who doubts is like a wave of the sea, blown and tossed by the wind. ⁷ That man should not think he will receive anything from the Lord; ⁸ he is a double-minded man, unstable in all he does. (James 1:5-6)

BEING WISE IS THE STATE OF BEING ONE WHO IS characterized by wisdom and marked by deep understanding, keen discernment and a capacity for sound judgment. Wise people are in high demand in our nation because wisdom is an invaluable resource. Being smart or intelligent is not as valuable as being wise because wisdom is the ability to correctly apply the knowledge that one has learned. Have you ever met a smart fool? They had all of the book knowledge in the world, but they lacked wisdom and common sense.

I am glad that God understands how important wisdom is. He left various examples of wisdom in the Scriptures as a guide for our lives: Proverbs, Ecclesiastes, Job and Songs of Solomon just to name a few. In addition to the written wisdom He provided in Scripture, God also writes a blank check of wisdom through James, the brother of Jesus. James said if we lack wisdom, all we need to do is put in a personal requisition through prayer asking for wisdom and God will give it generously without asking any questions. The only stipulation is that we must believe that we will receive wisdom when we ask for it.

When you think about it, God eliminates every excuse we might have to lack wisdom. I personally know that God will give you wisdom beyond your years, education and experience level. The all-wise God can and will give you all the wisdom you need, if you will ask. Later in his letter, James teaches us that we do not have some things because we do not ask. There are other things we do not have because we ask with the wrong motives. So, the first step to getting the wisdom you need is simply to ask God. When you ask, ask in faith believing that He will give it. The second step is to ask with the right motives. If you want wisdom so that you no longer need to depend on God, He probably will not grant that request. You would never consciously ask for autonomy, but often we want to know what we need to know to gain independence from God so we can do what needs to be done without having to come to Him time-after-time. God is in the business of keeping us dependent on Him. It is called faith.

So the question to ask yourself is in what area of your life do you need the wisdom of God? Have you asked for it? Do you need wisdom to know how to love your spouse or raise your children? Do you need wisdom to know how to start your own business or move up in your company? Do you need wisdom to lead a ministry or have a hard conversation with a friend? Where do you need God's wisdom? God has written a blank check, cash it! Write your needed area of wisdom on the amount line, sign your name in the paid to order line, and cash the check!

Now you are responsible for information that has been made available to you concerning wisdom. The wise choice would be to apply it in this moment by stopping to pray and ask God for the wisdom that you need. Take a moment to consider your request and then go before your Father with confidence knowing that He will give you the wisdom you are asking for.

Personal Reflection Questions

1. In what area of your life do you currently need the wisdom of God?

2. Reflect on a time when God has given you wisdom beyond your years, experience or education. What was the result?

3. Write your own personal prayer to God asking for the wisdom that you need.

Today's Prayer: *Lord, I thank you for the promise to give me the wisdom I need when I ask.   I am asking that you will give me the wisdom I need in the following areas in my life:*

_____

_____

_____

I am asking in faith and I pray that I will be open to receive the wisdom through whatever form you send it.

Statement of Being: Today, I will choose to be wise because I have access to all wisdom through God.

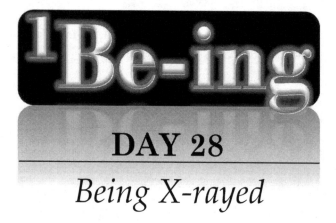

DAY 28

Being X-rayed

Main Entry: ¹x–ray
Pronunciation: \ˈeks-ˌrā \
Function: *transitive verb*
Definition: to examine, treat, or photograph with X-rays

[16] *Therefore confess your sins to each other and pray for each other so that you may be healed. The prayer of a righteous man is powerful and effective.* James 5:16

BEING "X-RAYED" IS THE STATE OF BEING ONE WHO IS examined, treated and photographed using radiation technology. X-rays have the ability to look beyond the surface to see inside of a person. Being X-rayed spiritually is choosing to live a life that is transparent so others will see you for who you really are. God has called each of us to be transparent in some way so that we can be healthy spiritually. The reason a person goes to the hospital to have an X-ray taken is because something is broken on the inside.

Similarly, in our spiritual journey, we need people in our lives that can function as a X-ray; that sees what is keeping us from being healthy on the inside.

Pride and fear often cause us to hide who we really are. Our pride says that we can handle our heart illnesses on our own and fear tells us that no one will accept us if they knew who we really were. We spend a great deal of our lives hiding from other people and lying to ourselves. The challenge with living life this way is that someone knows you are sick, but they are waiting for you to ask for help. The other challenge is that if we do not open up and allow someone in, we will die from the disease of secrecy and dishonesty. I want to encourage you to visit a friend that you can trust and invite them to be an x-ray. I want you to be open and share the areas of your life that need to heal.

Being X-rayed involves . . .

CONFESSING OUR SINS

Confession is one of the most powerful practices you can engage in as a believer. I know that it seems scary if you have never done it before, but once you experience the power of being open and confessing your sins to God, as well as confessing your sins to someone else you can trust, you will see the benefits immediately. The biblical definition of confession is "to say the same thing", so when we confess we are agreeing with God in that what He calls sin *is* sin, and we are agreeing that we *have* sinned. The freedom that comes from confession is invaluable to our spiritual journey. It keeps our hearts sensitive to God and it allows us to remain close to Him, as we are keeping a short account. Confessing to another person provides the positive peer pressure we need to resist sin. If I know that I am going to have to confess a sin in a weekly conversation with an accountability partner, my choice to sin becomes more costly and my desire to sin is curbed by my desire to share a good report instead of a challenging one during that time. The enemy loves to keep us in hiding through causing us to believe that if we share our real challenges, people will not receive us or respect us. This is Satan's form of deceit to make you and me the next Adam and Eve in the long lineage of his disreputable questioning of God's way.

PRAYING FOR ONE ANOTHER

After confessing, you want to engage in a time of prayer. Prayer invites God into the process of forgiving you for your sins so that you can be in right relationship with Him again. It also allows you to enlist the power of the Spirit to help you overcome the sin-struggle that you may have. Prayer also allows you to receive the love of someone else praying for you. There are few things that communicate God's love more effectively than the prayers of the righteous. James teaches us that the prayers of the righteous are powerful and effective, which means that when you pray from a right relationship with God, your prayers will work and you will see God answering them towards your freedom and deliverance.

BEING HEALED

Once you confess and pray you will experience the cathartic effects of confession. I remember the first time I shared my struggle with a close friend of mine. I was so afraid and so worried that he would reject me or judge me, but he prayed for me and continued to invite me to ask for his prayers. He also invited me into a mutually accountable relationship where we could consistently share with one another. After a while, I remember telling him that I thought God would ask me to share my struggle with a group of people one day and I felt that would be horrible. My friend was excited because he knew the healing power of confession for those who hear the confession and for those who confess. One year later, I was speaking at a conference and God led me to share my struggle and my confession encouraged many people who were there. He also used it to break the power of a sin-cycle in my life. He used confession to bring my challenge to the light. Once it was in the light, the power of it was gone. So, I share my story with you as a testimony of God's goodness and wisdom that provides confession and transparency as a means to bring us to healing. I encourage you to be transparent with someone you can trust and watch God work His healing power in your life.

Personal Reflection Questions

1. How are you transparent with God about your areas of struggle? Do you consistently confess sins to God in prayer?

2. What, if anything hinders you from being transparent with others?

3. If you were to begin being transparent with someone, who would you share with and what would you be willing to share in the first conversation?

Today's Prayer: *God, sometimes being transparent is challenging for me because I want to think I can handle struggling on my own, or I am afraid that I will be the only one who has the challenges that I have. Teach me to overcome fear with courage and to be open with someone about my areas of struggle because I do not want to suffer alone. I do not want to continue living as if my struggle does not exist. Help me to experience the healing power of confession and transparency.*

Statement of Being: Today, I will choose to be X-rayed because I want to be spiritually healthy.

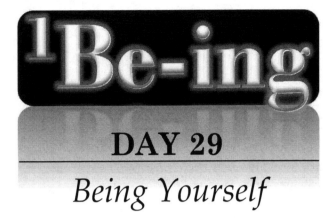

DAY 29

Being Yourself

Main Entry: ¹your·self
Pronunciation: \ yər-'self
Function: *pronoun*
Definition: that identical one that is you: your normal, healthy, or sane condition or self

¹³ *For you created my inmost being;*
   you knit me together in my mother's womb.
¹⁴ *I praise you because I am fearfully and wonderfully made;*
   your works are wonderful,
   I know that full well.
¹⁵ *My frame was not hidden from you*
   when I was made in the secret place.
When I was woven together in the depths of the earth,
   ¹⁶ *your eyes saw my unformed body.*
   All the days ordained for me
   were written in your book
   before one of them came to be.
   (Psalm 139:13-16)

BEING YOURSELF IS THE STATE OF BEING ONE WHO IS identical to the one that is you - the normal, healthy sane version of yourself. Have you ever heard someone say, "You just do not seem like yourself today?" They were speaking to the challenge that many individuals have to remain consistently themselves. Often, we change in order to be accepted or to fit in, but today I want to encourage you to be yourself.

David writes in Psalm 139 about the unique person that God has created each of us to be. He says that you are fearfully and wonderfully made. Being fearfully made means that when you were made, God was in awe of His creation in you. Just as we are in awe of God during moments of worship, God was in awe of you in the moment of creation. He looked at you with joy and pride knowing that the person He made was very good. Being wonderfully made means that you are wonderful not because of what you do, but because of who you are. God says so and that settles it. There is no one like you in the entire world and there never will be another, so you need to be yourself. Depending on your previous experiences, being yourself may not seem to be a wise decision, but being yourself is choosing to honor the wisdom of God in creating you. When you are yourself, people experience the benefit of being exposed to the gift that you are in their lives. I encourage you to put an imaginary bow on your head and walk out today with confidence knowing that you are a gift to the people who encounter you, as you are fearfully and wonderfully made by God.

Being yourself also involves living out the purpose for which God created you. The psalmist says that all the days ordained for you were written in God's book before one of them came to be. That means that God has a plan for your life, He has written it down and is watching in Heaven as His storyline for you is played out on the stage of life. I hope that you are excited about God's story in your life and I believe that each ending is going to be for His glory. So live according to the way God has formed you. Fully embrace who He has created you to be from your personality to your gifts and your passions. Embrace your family heritage and your experiences up to this point in your life. Allow the purpose of God to prevail in your life by being exactly who he made you to be . . . yourself.

Personal Reflection Questions

1. What is the next step for you to embrace being yourself?

2. Do you tend to be authentic when you are around other people, or do you tend to present a false self? Explain?

3. How is God challenging you to more fully live out your purpose in this season of your life?

Today's Prayer: *God, thank you for making me who I am. I know that there are things about me that I am still learning to embrace; there are other things that I love about me. Help me to see that all of who I am is who you created me to be. Help me to be myself so I can honor you with my life and bless others with the gift that I can be to them.*

Statement of Being: Today, I will be myself because I am fearfully and wonderfully made.

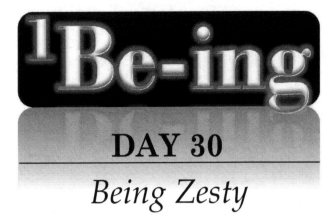

DAY 30

Being Zesty

Main Entry: ¹zesty
Pronunciation: \ˈzes-tē\
Function: *adjective*
Definition: having or characterized by zest: appealingly piquant or lively

¹³ *"You are the salt of the earth. But if the salt loses its saltiness, how can it be made salty again? It is no longer good for anything, except to be thrown out and trampled by men. (Matthew 5:13)*

BEING ZESTY IS THE STATE OF BEING SOMEONE WHO IS characterized by zest, appealingly piquant or lively. When is the last time you had a meal that was salty? Do you remember? Maybe someone put too much seasoning on the meat you had at a restaurant or someone put too much salt in the vegetables at a pot-luck dinner last week. Salt is zesty. It adds flavor to anything that it comes in contact with. Salt is also a preservative that was used in the New Testament day to preserve meat for long periods of time, as they did not have

Frigidaire deep freezers back then. Salt also has a way of making one thirsty after consuming it. The key to salt being effective in adding flavor, preserving meat or making someone thirsty is that salt must remain zesty. Once the salt lost its zest, it was no good; it would be thrown out and later walked on by people.

How is your zest for life? Do you find yourself being salty where people who come in contact with you have more flavors in their life when they leave your presence? I am not talking about just being outgoing; I am talking about having a lifestyle that is lively and attractive, one that causes others to thirst for the relationship you have with Christ. I am talking about having a zesty marriage that makes singles feel more excited about the possibility of wedded union. I am talking about having a zesty ministry that makes others want to serve as you serve. Jesus has declared that we are the salt of the earth and we have been given the mandate to be zesty Christians who add flavor and help to preserve others' saltiness around us. You and your friends should gain zest from conversations you have about what God is doing in your life, preserving your faith and your passion for God. The Bible says that we overcome by the blood of the Lamb and the word of our testimony. You can add zest to another life by simply sharing what God has done for you.

As we conclude our 30-day journey, I encourage you to be zesty and allow God to use you to add flavor to someone else's life. Be stimulating and allow God to use you to preserve another brother or sister in Christ. Be inspiring and allow God to use you to increase someone's thirst for Him. You can be zesty and make life more exciting for others.

Personal Reflection Questions

1. Who are some zesty people in your life that help preserve your faith? Take the time to let them know how much you appreciate their zest for a life in Christ.

2. Where do you need to gain more zest for your spiritual life at this season? How can you connect with another zesty person to increase your thirst for God in that area?

3. How can you personally add zest to the life of someone else today?

Today's Prayer: *Jesus, you called me the salt of the earth and I want to be salty. I want my zest for life to be so attractive that people want to come to know you and how you have impacted my life. Give me a zesty attitude today so I can preserve my brothers and sisters in Christ. I pray for a real thirst for you to be developed through a conversation I have today. Allow me to be zesty adding flavor to the life of someone else today.*

Statement of Being: Today, I will choose to be zesty because I am the salt of the earth.

Appendix

Your Daily Appointment with God

By Gaylon Clark and Corey Tabor

Many of us have meetings with important people throughout the day, but we often fear having a one-on-one meeting with God because we lack the knowledge, skills, and understanding of how to do so. In your daily appointment with God, you will learn how to arrange a meaningful meeting with the Maker through learning how to:

1. Give God Primetime
2. Get the Proper Tools
3. Grow through Prayer
4. Guard your Priority

Through these steps you can begin meeting with God today!

GIVE GOD PRIMETIME

Your daily appointment with God begins with giving him the prime time in your schedule. You want to meet with God when you are most ready, receptive, and responsive. For most people this time will be in the morning. As you honor Him with the first minutes of your day, He gives you wisdom with the remaining moments.

Psalm 5:3 - In the morning, O Lord, you hear my voice; in the morning I lay my requests before you and wait in expectation.

Mark 1:35 - very early in the morning, while it was still dark, Jesus got up, left the house and went off to a solitary place, where he prayed.

GET THE PROPER TOOLS

In order to have an effective meeting with God; it is important to get the proper tools that will prepare you for your appointment.

A) Get a newer translation of the Bible
B) Get a Devotional
C) Get Variety

Get a newer translation of the Bible

Often we struggle to read God's word because we are reading a version that is difficult to understand. When the King James Version was written in 1611, old English was the language of the day. Today the language that is being used is communicated through versions like the New International Version, or the New Living Translation. I also encourage you to consider getting a Life Application Study Bible that has historical notes, practical life applications, and study tools to help you better understand what you are reading.

Get a Devotional
Devotional Bibles have devotionals included. These Bibles can be purchased online at www.christianbook.com or at a local Christian bookstore.

Examples include:
- NIV Women's Devotional Bible
- New NIV Men's Devotional Bible
- NIV Couples Devotional Bible
- NIV Recover Devotional Bible
- NIV One Year Bible
- NIV Quiet Time Bible

Get Variety
In order to keep your time fresh with God, you might include reading Christian literature like, *The Purpose Drive Life* by Rick Warren, or *Too Busy Not to Pray* by Bill Hybels. There are a number of Christian books to help you grow in your walk with God.

GROW THROUGH PRAYER
1 Thessalonians 5:17 - pray continually;

Philippians 4:6 - Do not be anxious about anything, but in everything, by prayer and petition, with thanksgiving, present your requests to God. And the peace of God, which transcends all understanding, will guard your hearts and minds in Christ Jesus.

During your daily appointment with God, you want to include

moments to grow through prayer. Prayer is simply communicating with God. Through prayer, you are able to speak to God and allow Him to speak back to you. You can use the following approaches to assist you in your prayer life:

Develop a Prayer Menu
Develop a list of things you would like to pray for that day and write them down. You may want to pray through your schedule for the day or pray for particular things concerning you for that day. A prayer menu allows you to remain focused in your prayer time.

Establish a Prayer Schedule
A prayer schedule allows you to schedule days throughout the week to pray for particular areas in your life. You can create a prayer menu for each day in your prayer schedule. As people share their prayer requests, you can know you have days scheduled to pray for those particular requests.

The schedule below is an example of a prayer schedule.
- Sunday - Character (Pray for areas in your character that need to grow)
- Monday - Family (Immediate and extended)
- Tuesday - Church (Pastor, Leaders, Ministries, your role in the church)
- Wednesday-Neighbors (people that live in your community)
- Thursday – Friends
- Friday - Nation and the world (Leaders, Peace, Reconciliation)
- Saturday - Financial (personal giving, money management, debt, et)

Begin Praying Scripture

Praying Scripture is a great way to pray for wisdom to understand and apply what you have read in your devotional. You may pray scriptures related to promises from God or commands from God in Scripture. The Psalms are a great resource to pray the scriptures and express your heart to God. Finally, praying Scripture will assist you in praying for things that are within God's will.

Try Prayer Journaling

A prayer journal allows you to write out your prayers so you can focus as you pray. It also allows you to keep a record of what you have asked for. When God answers the prayer, you can mark that prayer as answered. Answered prayers increase our faith and energy for prayer in the future.

Share with a Prayer Partner

Praying with a prayer partner allows you to share particular requests with someone else that is in the community of faith and ask them to pray on your behalf while you are able to pray for their particular requests as well. The partnership helps you hold one another accountable in your walk with God. It can also provide the support you need to continue praying consistently. We usually encourage prayer partners to be the same gendered and to schedule a consistent time to pray together each week.

GUARD YOU PRIORITY

Once you have decided to prioritize your daily appointment with God, it will be important to guard it as your top priority.

Matthew 6:33 – But seek first His kingdom and His righteousness, and all these things will be given to you as well.

You can guard your priority to have a daily appointment with God through engaging in the following strategies:

Scheduling

Scheduling a consistent appointment with God encourages you to meet with Him consistently. You may commit to meeting with Him at 6:00 a.m. every morning before you prepare for work, or at 10:00 p.m. every evening before you go to bed. Scheduling it will solidify this priority in your life.

Sleep

Being sleepy can be a distraction to your time with God. You know your body and how much sleep you need to be alert in God's presence. In guarding your priority to meet with Him, it is important to plan your day so you can go to sleep at a decent hour to receive the rest you need.

Support

You may need to enlist additional support through a prayer partner to ask you how you are doing in keeping your daily appointment with God. Knowing that you will need to answer questions about your time with God each week will provide you with additional support to keep your appointment with God.

Space

Part of guarding your priority to meet with God involves finding a space that you can associate with your daily appointment with God. It may be a room in your house, a chair in your office, or a park in your neighborhood. Having a specific place will help you mentally relocate into God's presence.

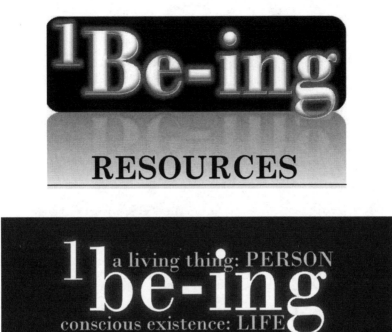

Book – Order an additional copy of *¹be-ing* for a friend or family member. (ISBN – 13: 978-0-9819377-0-0)

Audio Book – Enjoy the convenience of listening to your *¹be-ing* devotional in your car or on your mp3 player.
(ISBN – 13: 978-0-9819377-2-4)

E-Book – Enjoy the convenience of reading your *¹be-ing* devotional on your laptop or PDA.
(ISBN – 13: 978-0-9819377-1-7)

T-Shirt –Wear your new identity with your own *¹be-ing* t-shirt.

To order additional *¹be-ing* resources go to
www.iiicoaching.com

COACHING™

This is what we speak, not in words taught us by human wisdom but in words taught by the Spirit, expressing spiritual truths in spiritual words.
1 Corinthians 2:13

Mission: To inform, instruct and inspire people and organizations to fulfill their God-given purpose.

Method: III Coaches inform, instruct and inspire people and organizations through conferences, seminars, workshops, and various media outlets.

Membership: If you have are a gifted communicator or ministry leader looking to use your gifts to inform, instruct and inspire, join us as a III Coach as we partner with you to build and equip the body of Christ.

Ministry: To book a III Coach for your next event go to www.iiicoaching.com or call (877) 893-1911.

III Coaching, LLC
P.O. Box 972
Cedar Park, Texas 78630
(877) 893-1911
www.iiicoaching.com

About the Author

 Corey Tabor serves as the Maturity and Ministry Pastor at Greater Mt. Zion Baptist Church in Austin, Texas where he oversees membership, discipleship and adult ministries under the leadership of Lead Pastor Gaylon Clark.

Corey is also the Founder and President of III Coaching, LLC a coaching firm that specializes in ministry coaching and life purpose coaching.

Prior to coming on staff at Greater Mt. Zion, Corey served as the Founder and Campus Staff Member of Texas Gospel Fellowship with InterVarsity Christian Fellowship at the University of Texas at Austin, growing the ministry to over 130 students in just four years.

Corey graduated from the University of Texas at Austin in August of 2000 with a B.S. in Communication Studies / Human Relations and a minor in Business. He is currently pursuing a Masters of Divinity degree at Rockbridge Seminary.

Corey's dynamic speaking style connects with people from various backgrounds and his passion for racial reconciliation and multi-ethnic ministry leads him to speak to various groups and organizations.

Corey has been the proud husband of April Tabor since June 7, 2003. They married after nearly four years of dating and serving together in ministry. April serves as the Children's Director at Greater Mt. Zion Baptist Church. Corey and April currently live in Cedar Park, Texas.

Book Corey for an upcoming event at www.coreytabor.com